YOU CAN TEACH YOURSELF®
COUNTRY GUITAR

by Dix Bruce

CD Contents

This book is available either by itself or packaged with a companion audio and/or video recording. If you have purchased the book only, you may wish to purchase the recordings separately. The publisher strongly recommends using a recording along with the text to assure accuracy of interpretation and make learning easier and more enjoyable.

2 3 4 5 6 7 8 9 0

© 2003 BY MEL BAY PUBLICATIONS, INC., PACIFIC, MO 63069.

Visit us on the Web at www.melbay.com — E-mail us at email@melbay.com

PREFACE

Dix Bruce is a musician, writer and award-winning guitar player from the San Francisco Bay Area. He edited **Mandolin World News** from 1978 to 1984, and has recorded two albums with bluegrass legend Frank Wakefield. He recently completed a solo folk recording, *My Folk Heart,* and has just released a band recording of string swing & jazz, *Tuxedo Blues,* with many of his original compositions. He is a columnist for the Fretted Instrument Guild of America newsletter, was a frequent contributor to **FRETS** magazine, and writes for **Acoustic Guitar**. He has taught mandolin, guitar, and bass for nearly twenty years.

Also by Dix Bruce:

Beginning Country Guitar Handbook/tape (Mel Bay) teaches all the basics of flatpicking country guitar: chords, backup, bass runs, leads, bluegrass picking, introductory music theory, soloing & improvisation, how to use a capo, how to transpose, and much more. Includes eighteen great traditional American folk/country songs with lyrics. Stereo tape has all book songs and examples at slow & regular speeds.

Back Up Trax – A series of play-along book & tape sets. Learn melodies and practice soloing and improvising by playing along with great rhythm sections. Each melody from the book is recorded at slow speed (with just guitar accompaniment) and regular speed (with whole band), then the band plays several choruses of the tune while you supply the melody or solo! Stereo cassette tapes allow you to isolate recorded melodies from rhythm section for study. Repeat a song, at either speed, as many times as you wish, perfecting phrases, melodies, and solos in a band context – they'll jam all night long! Beginners can practice basic skills, while more advanced players can hone their improvisational chops – each at their own individual learning rates. You'll be amazed at your progress. Here's what's currently available:

Back Up Trax: Old Time & Fiddle Tunes Vol. 1 (Mel Bay) Learn melodies and practice soloing on fourteen of the most popular old time & fiddle tunes: *Temperance Reel, Sally Goodin, Blackberry Blossom, Over the Waves, Beaumont Rag, Red Haired Boy, June Apple, Salty Dog, The Wayfaring Stranger, Black Mountain Rag, Arkansas Traveller, Soldier's Joy, Billy in the Lowground* and *Old Joe Clark.* Available in two editions: fiddle/mandolin with mandolin tablature, and guitar/banjo with guitar and banjo tablature.

Back Up Trax: Swing & Jazz (Mel Bay) Great string rhythm section: guitar, mandolin, & bass. Learn solos and practice melodies and improvisation on twelve of the most played standard progressions in swing & jazz: two-five-one, one-six-two-five or cycle of fifths, major blues, minor blues, and much more. Two editions: one for guitar, mandolin, violin and other strings and one for reed and horn players. You supply the lead. We'll play all night long!

Back Up Trax: Traditional Jazz & Dixieland (Mel Bay) Play-along book & tape set featuring traditional jazz rhythm section — banjo, tuba, piano & drums with trumpet leads. Learn melodies and practice improvising on the most popular traditional jazz and Dixieland tunes (*Saints, Down by the Riverside, Bill Bailey, St. James Infirmary, Just a Closer Walk, St. Louis Blues, Frankie & Johnnie,* 16 in all). All tunes on tape at slow & regular speed. You supply the lead. We'll play all night long!

You Can Teach Yourself Mandolin (Mel Bay) book/tape covers chords, strums, tuning, basic note reading, tremolo, and loaded with 19 well-known, easy songs for the beginning mandolinist. Stereo tape has all book songs and examples at slow & regular speeds.

All of the above are available from Mel Bay Publications, Inc., P.O. Box 66, Pacific, MO 63069.

Extra special thanks to Duane Wong of The Music Works, El Cerrito, CA, Jim Nunally, and Annie Johnston for their invaluable help and suggestions.

TABLE OF CONTENTS

INTRODUCTION

This book and tape set will teach you all the basics of country guitar: chords, strums, picking patterns, basic backup, accompaniment and flatpicking, how to transpose (play a song in a different key), how to use a capo, an explanation of the "Nashville Number" system of chords, and much more, all demonstrated on well-known folk and country classics (along with a few brand-new country songs) and recorded at slow and regular speeds on the accompanying cassette tape. You'll learn what all the country greats learned when they were beginners. Work at your own pace and discover the joys of country guitar technique from the Original Carter Family, Jimmie Rogers, Merle Haggard, Rosanne Cash, Emmy Lou Harris, and George Jones to the hot new sounds of artists like Garth Brooks, Wynonna Judd, Ricky Skaggs, Kathy Mattea, Vince Gill, Trisha Yearwood, Clint Black, Randy Travis, Mary Chapin-Carpenter, Travis Tritt, Patty Loveless, and more.

Our first objective is to learn all the important major, minor, and seventh chords. We'll take them a couple at a time and learn them in the context of simple songs that you are probably already familiar with. Once you know them, these chords can be used on any song in any style of music. The fact is, if you learn just a handful of chords (no pun intended!), say five or six, you'll have the basic tools to play just about every country, rock, or popular song you've ever heard. The majority of country songs are even simpler — usually having only two to four chords.

The songs we'll use to learn chords are mostly traditional American country and folk songs. As you learn them, you'll accomplish our second objective which is to give you a repertoire to exercise your chords and technique. As I mentioned above, we use these classic songs mainly because you are likely to be somewhat familiar with them. It's a bit easier to learn chords and strums on songs you know. Also, there are so many wonderful traditional songs out there that you should be aware of. They are the heart and soul of our American heritage, and are the well from which current country springs.

Our third objective is to teach you several accompaniment techniques that you can lift from these songs and apply to the latest songs on the country charts or to things that you've written. As I write these words, country music is the most popular music in the U.S.A. It may be this new popularity that led you to an interest in learning country guitar. If so, you may be more interested in current country than traditional country. That's fine — every chord and strum you learn in this book (and many of the songs) will be useful to you in current country music situations. After all, a G chord is a G chord, a bass-strum pick is a bass-strum pick, an arpeggio pick is an arpeggio strum no matter what tune or style of music you find it in! (We'll explore all of these in the book.) After you've learned a few songs and strums in this book, head for the music store and buy a songbook with your favorite singer's music in it. Take what you're learning here and apply it to other situations. You'll be amazed at how much fun you'll have.

One important point: SING! About 99% of what's in the book and on the tape is oriented toward accompanying vocal music. You need to learn to accompany yourself first as preparation for accompanying others. If you're shy, close the door and draw the curtains. Your voice doesn't have to sound like Emmy Lou Harris or Merle Haggard, it just has to sound like you. Maybe it's a little rough or out of tune, loud or soft, high or low, but who cares? Throw your head back and let fly! Always sing and play along with me on the tape. There will be times when the song is pitched too high or low. In these cases do the best you can. We'll learn how to accommodate different voices in the course of the book.

The accompanying stereo cassette is highly recommended. It's a great teach-yourself aid and will help you learn very quickly. On it I demonstrate every strum and technique and play every song, most at two speeds: very slow and at regular speed. The slow demonstrations will let you hear what's being described on the printed page. If you don't read music, don't panic, you'll be able to hear how every song goes on the tape. Sometimes a five-second demonstration can take the place of hundreds of words. And, once you can play a little bit, you can jam along with the tape to hone your chops! Fast versions of most songs have a contemporary country rhythm section with bass and drums, so it's just like playing along with a band.

So, these are our three main objectives: learn all the common chords, practice these chords on a bunch of songs and in the process learn a repertoire, and use these songs and chords to master different accompaniment techniques. Along the way we'll learn about the other things mentioned above: basic backup, beginning flatpicking and fingerpicking, how to transpose, how to use a capo, an explanation of the "Nashville Number" system of chords and other useful tidbits of information that will help you **Teach Yourself Country Guitar**.

Dix Bruce – 1993

Photo by Rob Thomas

ABOUT THE GUITAR

Before we get into our first chords, songs and strums, let's talk a bit about the guitar. The diagram below shows a generic guitar with its various parts labeled. Yours probably won't look exactly like this, but it should look more like this than, say, a vacuum cleaner. This is a basic flat top guitar. Electrics, archtops, and classical guitars have slight differences, but all have strings and make noise. Refer to this diagram as we progress through the text.

THE GUITAR AND ITS PARTS

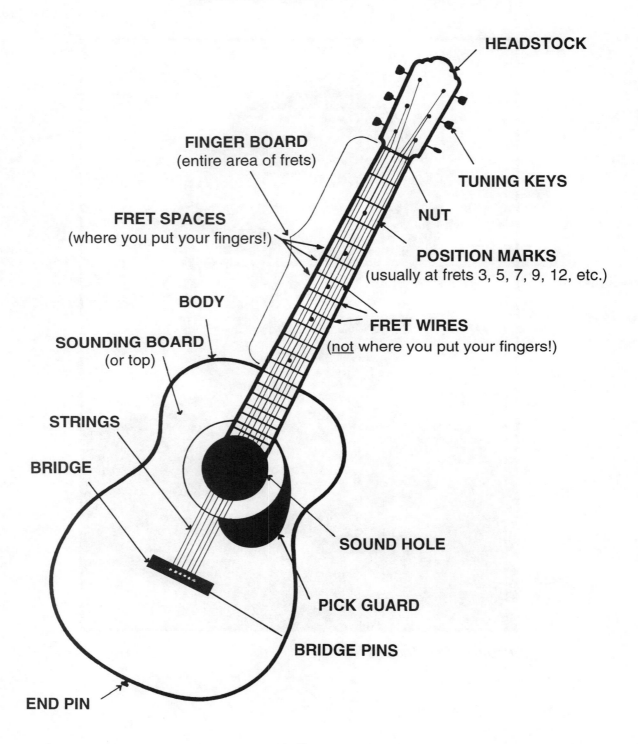

HEADSTOCK

FINGER BOARD
(entire area of frets)

TUNING KEYS

FRET SPACES
(where you put your fingers!)

NUT

POSITION MARKS
(usually at frets 3, 5, 7, 9, 12, etc.)

BODY

FRET WIRES
(not where you put your fingers!)

SOUNDING BOARD
(or top)

STRINGS

BRIDGE

SOUND HOLE

PICK GUARD

BRIDGE PINS

END PIN

Any type of guitar will work fine, steel or nylon string, acoustic or electric. You might want to try out a few different types and brands to see what you like best. If you are a beginner, try to find a guitar that's relatively easy to play, although that's hard to determine right now since you may not play at all and everything seems difficult! Nylon-stringed guitars are usually a bit easier on the fingers, but steel-stringed guitars are louder and more the norm in country music, especially for playing rhythm or backup, which is the major focus of **You Can Teach Yourself Country Guitar**. (Willie Nelson is one country star who always plays his faithful nylon-stringed guitar, which he flatpicks. Next time you see him, notice that his fingers have worn a hole right in the top of it! Don't be afraid of trying flatpicks on a nylon-stringed guitar.) As you play and learn, you'll develop a more focused idea of your sound and that will determine your ultimate choice of guitar brand and type.

The strings should be relatively close to the fingerboard but not buzz on the frets when you strum the strings, fretted or open, and the instrument should sound pleasant. Make sure the neck isn't warped and that the instrument has no cracks. You may need the advice of a more experienced player to help you find that first good guitar. Keep in mind that it doesn't need to be perfect, just playable.

Consider a used instrument. Looks should be your last consideration. (See note on Willie Nelson's guitar above.) Don't spend a fortune on the instrument — you don't yet know what you like. I personally love Martins and Gibsons. They're expensive, but they tend to hold their value. There are several lower priced lines that are perfect for beginners including Takamine, Alvarez, Fender, Washburn, Ibanez, Hohner, Saga, Ovation and Yamaha. Most music stores also rent guitars and this can provide you the perfect opportunity to examine and play an instrument at your leisure. It's very difficult to evaluate a guitar in the public hubbub of a store. The best music stores will apply rental fees, sometimes up to 100%, toward purchase of an instrument, and that's a pretty good deal.

Be sure to get a case. Gig bags are light and easy to carry and, though they are padded, provide very little protection for the guitar. Chipboard (basically fancy cardboard) cases are cheap and offer a bit more protection than a gig bag. Hardshell cases are heavy, more expensive, but provide the most protection from bumps, scratches, and weather. However, even hardshell cases and their precious contents can quickly be turned into splinters by the airline gorillas.

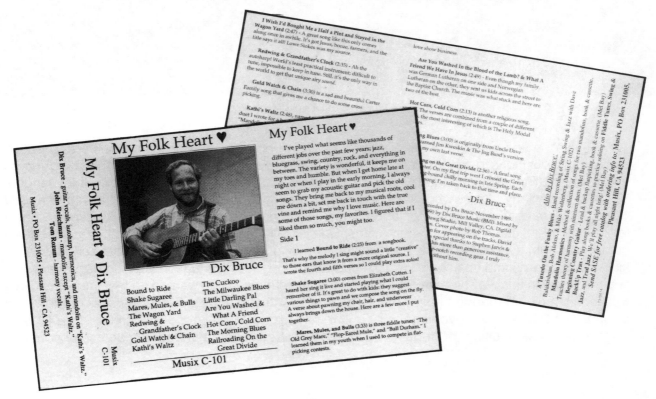

HOW TO HOLD THE GUITAR

The photos below show how to hold the guitar. Use these as a guide and try to find a relaxed position that's comfortable for you. You'll be playing for hours at a time so this is important. When sitting, I find it best to elevate my right leg slightly (either by crossing my legs or by using a small foot stool,) and place the guitar's waist on it, especially if you don't use a strap. I recommend that you use a guitar strap whenever you play, either in the sitting or standing position. Sometimes it's difficult for students to make the transition from sitting to standing. Use of a strap from the beginning can ease this transition.

Photos by Kathi Bruce

The photos also show general arm and hand placement. The main rule here is to find comfortable positions to play in. Most of you will strum and pick with your right hand, and hold chords with your left. If you're left handed, you have a few options. The most obvious is to play right handed. Virtually every lefty I know who plays guitar does it right handed. It's simpler in this right-handed world. If you're politically conscious about your left-handedness, (that is, you think of yourself as a leftist) you might consider other alternatives. One is to flip the guitar and play it with the headstock out to your right. Of course in this position you'll have to read all the chord diagrams and tablature kind of backwards and upside down. To moderate this confusing situation a bit, some players who flop the guitar in this way also reverse the order of the strings. If you want to do that you should buy a specially built left-handed guitar that is braced to withstand the different tension of the string arrangement. Otherwise, over time, your guitar may fold up like a potato chip. In this book I'll refer to your hands as "picking" or "fretting" so I have all bases covered and won't confuse anyone!

8

Keep the elbow and wrist of the fretting hand relaxed. The thumb should lie loosely on the back of the guitar neck. To make chords, you'll squeeze the neck and strings with your fretting fingers and thumb. (Here's where that opposable thumb really comes in handy. That's why you have to be at least a monkey on the evolutionary chain to play guitar. Let's not talk about the steel guitar — don't get me started.) The trick is to use as little pressure as possible to get a clear, ringing tone. That's why you want a guitar that has low action (strings that are easy to press to the fretboard). Arch your fingers slightly above the strings so the very tips of your fingers contact the strings. We number each fretting-hand finger as follows: #1 = index, #2 = middle, #3 = ring, #4 = pinkie, T = thumb. We'll discuss this in greater detail when we get to chord diagrams.

I tend to pick the strings, whether I'm using my thumb, my fingers, or a flatpick, over the soundhole nearer the bridge than the end of the fingerboard. More on that later.

TUNING THE GUITAR

The most difficult thing beginning guitar players have to face is tuning their guitar. Have faith and realize that it's a skill that will, in time, be mastered. Tuning involves matching the sound of the strings to a reference note. This can be any sound source; a tuning fork, a pitch pipe, a piano, the accompanying cassette tape, another guitar or instrument, an electronic tuner, even a loud electric fan! (Just joking.) Loosening a string by adjusting its tuning gear lowers the string's pitch, tightening a string raises its pitch. If you're new to music or the guitar, you'll probably need the help of a more advanced player or teacher to get you started with tuning.

The guitar has six strings tuned to different pitches. String 1 (highest pitched and thinnest) is tuned to E, string 2 to B, string 3 to G, string 4 to D, string 5 to A, and string 6 to E two octaves below string 1. If you look a guitar in the face, as in "The Guitar and Its Parts" diagram, string 1 (highest pitched and thinnest) is far right, string 6 (lowest pitched and thickest) is far left. As you hold the guitar in playing position, the low E string (string 6, lowest pitched and thickest) is closest to your head, the high E string (string 1, highest pitched and thinnest) closest to your knee. To remember the string names 1 to 6 (highest pitched to lowest) think "Every Boy Gets Dinner At Eight." The diagram below shows where these notes are located on the piano keyboard.

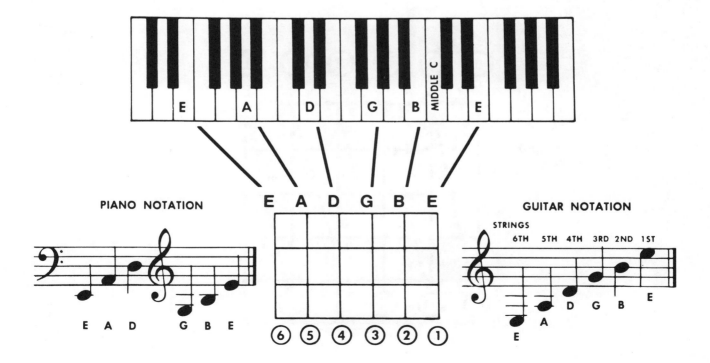

9

For the purposes of working with this book, I suggest that you tune to the tones at the beginning of the cassette. This will put you in tune with the taped examples and allow you to play along. Some of you lucky souls will have cassette players with speed/pitch controls that allow you to tune the machine to your instrument. Beware though, you'll still have to put your guitar in tune with itself. Read on.

If you have trouble distinguishing and matching pitches, electronic tuners can help by giving you a visual cue when a string is in tune. This can save you a lot of frustration as you begin developing tuning skills. Just make sure that you don't get addicted to tuners or you may never develop the very necessary skill of manual tuning. Also be aware that most electronic tuners are designed to be used with electric instruments. As such, these marvels of computer technology don't usually work well with acoustic guitars. You can get a small contact mike with a rubber suction cup to stick to your instrument and plug into the tuner while you tune. Try before you buy. If it won't work in the store, it won't work at home or on the gig.

Once you've tuned to the tape or another source, you'll need to fine tune your guitar to itself. First make sure that your sixth string, low E, is at the correct source pitch by tuning to a piano, electronic tuner, pitch pipe, etc. Fret the sixth string at the fifth fret. Match the sound of the open fifth-string A to this pitch by raising or lowering the pitch of the open A string, **not the E!**, by turning the tuning gear of the fifth-string A. Once that's done you have the E and A, sixth and fifth strings, in tune. Next fret the fifth-string A at the fifth fret and match the open fourth-string D sound to it the same way you did with the sixth and fifth strings, by turning the tuning gear of the fourth-string D. Next, fret the fourth-string D at the fifth fret and match the open third-string G sound to it. Now it gets tricky. Fret the third string G at the **fourth** fret and match the open second-string B to it. (This is the one snafu in the otherwise regular tuning arrangement of the guitar. It's confusing and tough to remember, but learn it proudly with the knowledge that it distinguishes our guitar from lesser stringed instruments like banjos and fiddles.) Finally, fret the second-string B at the fifth fret and match the open first-string E to it. Ta-da! All six strings will be perfectly in tune! Well maybe. Be patient, you'll probably have to practice this a bit. It's a good idea to check your tuning with this method before each playing session. The diagram below graphically illustrates this process.

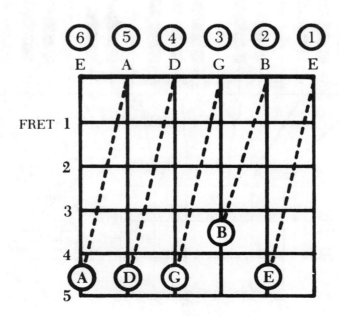

CHORD DIAGRAMS

Chord diagrams, like those below, are graphic representations of the guitar fingerboard and they tell you where to put the fingers of your fretting hand. Vertical lines represent the strings, 1 to 6, right to left, high E to low E. Horizontal lines represent frets, and the numbers inside the grid show which fingers are used to fret the strings. Look at the hand diagram below and note finger numbers: 1-index, 2-middle, 3-ring, 4-pinkie, T-thumb.

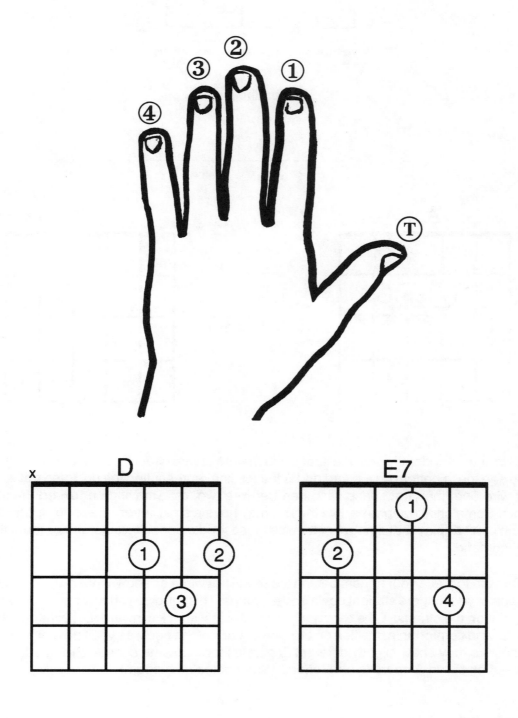

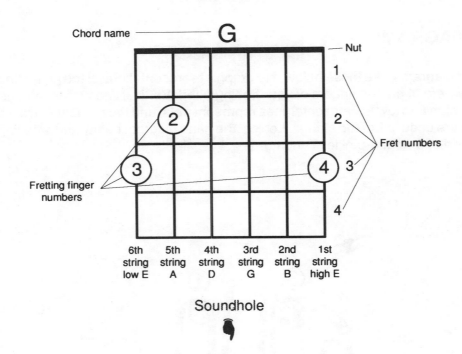

Headstock

Chord name ——————— G

Nut

1

2 — Fret numbers

3

4

Fretting finger numbers

6th string low E 5th string A 4th string D 3rd string G 2nd string B 1st string high E

Soundhole

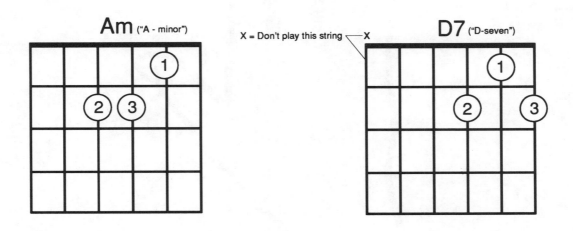

Am ("A - minor")

X = Don't play this string — X

D7 ("D-seven")

Fret numbers identify both the space and metal fret wire directly below them on the diagram. What you see top to bottom on a chord grid is the top line representing the nut, then fret space one, then fret wire one, then fret space two, then fret wire two, etc., moving on toward the imaginary soundhole. Some chord diagrams, like the D7, may have a small letter "x" above certain strings to let you know not to play that string. Try to miss these x-ed strings as you strum or mute them with your fretting hand.

Be sure to place your fingers behind the metal fret wires as shown, not *on* them. Always use the very *tips* of your fingers straight down on the strings. This will give you a strong and manageable contact point on the strings. Take care not to bend the first knuckle inward. Let your thumb seek its own natural and comfortable position on the side or back of the neck, as you finger different chords. Different books may show slightly different fingerings for the same chords. Pick the fingering you like best—after all, an A chord is an A chord! (See photos next page.)

Photos by Kathi Bruce

As you first practice new chords, pick each string individually to isolate any buzzes or dead spots that might arise from improperly placed fingertips. When you hear problems, try adjusting your grip until they are improved. There will be frustrating times when one finger/string combination buzzes. When that's fixed, another string that's supposed to sound is muted. When you correct that, the buzz comes back! Give it some time and effort and eventually you'll discover the right combination of position and pressure to make the chord sound great. Also realize that, just like an athlete, there will be a certain amount of soreness in your hand and arm muscles and fretting fingertips as they develop. This is quite normal and shouldn't hold you back. If it's <u>very</u> painful, you're probably doing something <u>very</u> wrong and you should seek the professional advice of a doctor and good music teacher. A certain amount of soreness, especially in your fingertips, is normal and the more you play, even with the soreness, the quicker callouses will form and soreness will vanish.

THE D AND A7 CHORDS

The first chords you'll learn are the D and A7.

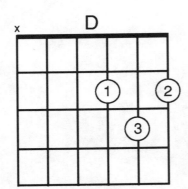

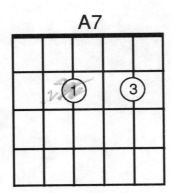

Let's introduce ourselves to the new D and A7 chords with a simple strum exercise. You should play through this exercise with every group of new chords you learn to get used to changing from one to the other. Make the D chord, and strum even downstrokes with your thumb or a flatpick. The naked thumb is going to be easier than holding a flatpick at this point, but you should prepare yourself for the eventuality of having to learn to use a pick. Buy a few different shapes and gauges of picks (forget thin picks, stick to mediums or heavys), and start flailing away with them. Keep them in your pocket at all times. (They're great for puncturing the tight plastic shrink wrap on CDs and cassettes.) What you want to be able to do is hold the chord, strum the pattern (in this case simple down strokes) clean and clear, and keep the pattern going without slowing down or stopping as you change chords. That's not easy! The key is to play the exercise as slowly as you need to in order to change the chords smoothly and not lose the rhythm of your strum. The rhythm and feel of the music is more important than anything else. Listen to the exercise on the tape.

If you're like me and everybody else I know, you're going to pretty much ignore those last few sentences. On the other hand, if you do as I suggest and play slow enough to change smoothly, you're probably that one person in a million who can leave the last ragged piece of brownie in the pan or turn away from that last chocolate-chip cookie on the plate. If this is the case, you have too much self-control and may not be cut out to be a musician! It's very tempting to push ahead and play fast once you can hold a chord and strum a bit. The hard part is changing from the chord you're holding to another. You have to give your fingers and brain a little time to learn the moves. That's what the exercise is designed to do. If you use it, you'll find the songs will come a bit easier. It's better to use up your frustration quotient on a stupid exercise than on a song. So, swat it out on the exercise! If you can play it as written, try changing chords after only two strums, then one.

In the exercise below, strums are indicated by slashes (/). They're grouped in fours, and each four strums is a measure. You can keep track of where you are in the measure by counting "one — two — three — four" as you play. Each group of four strums or counts is separated by a vertical line (|) called a measure or bar line. Many of the songs we'll learn will have four strums or beats in each measure. Others will have three beats, and these are waltzes. You may also come across songs with two or six beats to the measure but these can be thought of as variations of four- and three-beat measures.

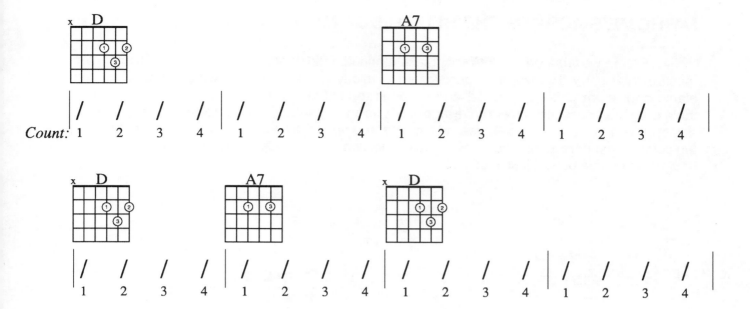

When you play a *chord* you're playing several *notes* at the same time. Different notes give us different-sounding chords. Chord names (A, D7, Gm, F diminished, B♭ minor, E♭ minor seven flat five, C augmented, E thirteen), define these combinations of notes, and similar names denote similar types of chords. The D and A chords sound very different but they are two chords of the same type — *major triads*. Dm ("D minor") and Am ("A minor") sound very different from their major siblings and from each other, but the Dm and Am are of the same type — *minor triads*. This holds true for D7 ("D seven" or "D seventh") and A7 ("A seven" or "A seventh") — referred to as dominant seventh chords. These three chord types — major, minor and dominant seven — are the three types found most often in country music. The Chord Dictionary at the back of this book shows all the common chords of this type.

So, practice making the D and the A7 chords and changing between them. When you can do it with ease, proceed to the first song. (Think of this as your first step up the stairway to the Grand Old Opry stage!)

Advanced accompaniment patterns on cassette tape:

My Home's Across the Blue Ridge Mountains — Bass note brush

Handsome Molly — Bass note brush

I Ride an Old Paint — Double arpeggio fingerpick

Red River Valley — Bass note brush

Shady Grove — Arpeggio fingerpick

Home on the Range — Bass note brush, key of C capoed @ fret 5

Going Down This Road Feeling Bad — Bass note brush w/ connectors

The Cuckoo — Bass note brush w/ fingers

I Get Blue — Lead

Some Drink — Bass note brush w/fingers

Children Go Where I Send Thee — muffled backbeat

Joshua Fought the Battle of Jericho — ////

Don't The Road Look Rough & Rocky? — Bass note brush w/fingers

Fair & Tender Ladies — /\/\/\

In The Pines — Bass note brush w/fingers

The House of the Rising Sun — /\/\/\//

Nobody Sleeps at My Place — //// swingy

Devil's Dream — Bass note brush

Darling You're a Fool — /\/\

MY HOME'S ACROSS THE BLUE RIDGE MOUNTAINS

Before we work on our first song, take a minute to look at the excerpt below. The printed music in this book will show you a song's chords, melody, lyrics, the key it's written in, tape counter blank, and strum pattern. (The advanced songs toward the end of the book will also include tablature.) Most cassette players have tape counters and these can be very useful in finding specific selections on the tape. To use it, rewind the tape and reset the counter to zero. Then, write down the counter numbers at the beginning of each selection in the space provided on the sheet music. I suggest you use pencil, just in case.

It's important that you work through all the verses to every song. Extra verses are presented immediately after the music. The more you exercise your fingers and golden throat, the faster you'll memorize chords and songs. Play along with the tape. (There may be instances on the tape where longer songs are shortened due to time restrictions. On your own, you should still play through entire songs.) Repetition is your best teacher and in no time you'll have the chords memorized. Be patient, it might not sound much like country music to you right now, just give it time.

The first song, *My Home's Across the Blue Ridge Mountains*, uses the D and A7 chords. The strum is even, single downstrokes. Assuming that your guitar is tuned correctly, the starting note for the melody you sing is an A, played on the third string at the second fret. Listen to the versions on the tape; start with the slow version. When you can play along with me on that, try the regular-speed version. As you listen and play along with the tape, you'll notice that it's in stereo and that there are often two different styles of playing heard, one on the right channel, one on the left. On one channel you'll hear straight chord strums, on the other channel the more advanced accompaniment. By adjusting the balance of your stereo, you'll be able to isolate each and focus on one or the other. For now, concentrate on the simple strums. We'll get back to more advanced things later on in the book. Fast versions of most of the songs have bass and drums added so you really feel what it's like to play in a country band. (See page 15 for a listing of these advanced accompaniment patterns.)

A few pages back, I mentioned that after you know a few chords, you should seek out songbooks of your favorite artists and songs. Get in the habit of swapping songs with friends. Transcribe lyrics from records or the radio. However you do it, immerse yourself in the music. You'll often find lyrics in songbooks and magazines written without music. Sometimes the chords are included, sometimes they aren't. In any case, you need to get used to this form. Below the standard music for *My Home's Across the Blue Ridge Mountains,* you'll find extra verses to the song along with chord letters and strum markings. This song lends itself especially well to making up your own verses. Doing that can extend the song, make you feel more like it's your own, and give you extra practice. The song is alternately known as *My Home's Across the Smoky Mountains.* You could substitute just about any location: *Deep Blue Water, Great Wide Valley, Midwest Prairie*, etc. Here in Northern California we could say *My Home's Across the Nimitz Freeway*. That brings up another point: Country is less of an actual location than it is a state of mind. You folks in New York City keep on pickin' and singin'!

My Home's Across
the Blue Ridge Mountains

Traditional - Key of D

Chorus: My home's a - cross the Bl - ue Ri - dge Moun - tains, My
1. Rock my ba - by feed him can - dy,

home's a - cross the Blue Ridge Mou - n - tains, My
Rock my ba - by feed him can - dy,

home's a - cross the Bl - ue Ri - dge Moun - tains, And I
Rock my ba - by feed him can - dy, And I

ne - ver ex - pect to see you an - y more.
ne - ver ex - pect to see you an - y more.

D
How can I keep from cry - ing?

A7   **D**
How can I keep from cry - ing?

D
How can I keep from cry - ing? And I

A7   **D**
never ex - pect to see you any - more.

D
I'm going back to North Carolina
A7   **D**
I'm going back to North Carolina
D
I'm going back to North Carolina
     A7   **D**
And I never expect to see you anymore.

You'll need to memorize chords and be able to play them without the help of chord diagrams. The only way that will happen is if you play a lot. By yourself, with friends, along with me on the tape, PRACTICE. Every time you learn new chords, songs and strums, go back over the old material. Find new material with the same chords and strums. Exercise your fingers, mind and voice.

HANDSOME MOLLY, A & E7 CHORDS, THE FLATPICK

Handsome Molly needs two new chords, the A and the E7, shown below.

A

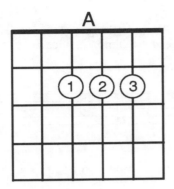

E7

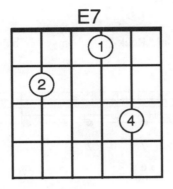

Now it's time to dive into flatpicking full force! You should have several flatpicks of medium or heavy stiffness in your jeans pocket. Fish a couple of them out and start playing the guitar with them. (By the way, some players make a lot of noise about how great real tortoise-shell picks are and that they can't play with anything but. You're new to all of this so please stick to plastic picks. Real tortoise picks are difficult to get, they're illegal to import into and sell in the U.S. {your music store probably won't sell them over the counter}, they're expensive, very thick and hard, and tortoises give their lives for them. I've tried them and the sound is not right for me, so I guess it's easy for me to say all of this. Still, it seems a shame to put a species' survival in jeopardy for flatpicks.) Check out the photos below which show how I hold the pick.

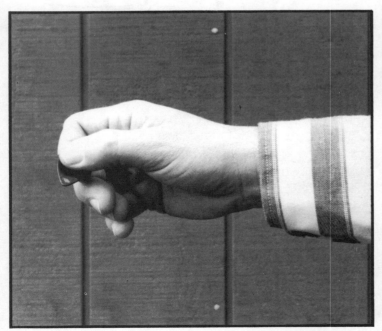 

Photos by Kathi Bruce

If you're not used to holding a flatpick, be patient. No doubt it'll fly out of your hand now and then at the least opportune moments. Your hand may also cramp up until you find just the right amount of pressure to hold it securely. Don't squeeze it too tightly. Again, be patient. Your pick grip is crucial to everything you play. Since I can't be there with you physically, it might be worth your while to enlist some in-person, teacher advice to get you started on the right foot, or in this case, the right hand!

When I strum, the fourth finger of my right hand brushes the pickguard on the guitar. When I pick continuous melody notes, I loosely anchor my fourth finger on the pickguard. Many players don't anchor their picking hand at all, and pivot from the wrist and/or elbow. Over time you'll develop your own approach, but for now experiment with both and concentrate on finding a comfortable position. If it hurts, you're doing something wrong. Hold the pick firmly, but without tension. My friend Frank Wakefield, the great bluegrass mandolinist, recommends a very loose and limber picking-hand wrist for both guitar and mandolin. He characterizes the motion as "letting your wrist shake your hand."

I tend to pick the strings over the soundhole nearer the bridge than the end of the fingerboard. I change this hand position to slightly alter the sound; moving toward the fingerboard gives me a mellow sound, toward the bridge a punchier, more trebly sound. Before you try to play *Handsome Molly*, work through the new chord exercise several times. Use the single down strum again, which can be challenging while you're trying to hold a flatpick.

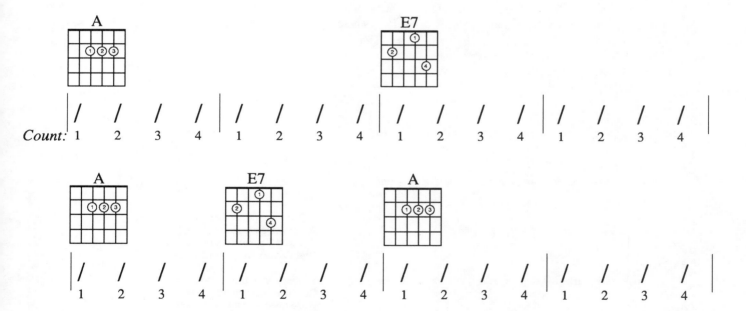

Again, play through all the verses. You'll have to be able to transfer the strum from above — in this case it should be fairly easy since it's a simple down strum — and be able to remember chords when you see their letter names and not the diagrams. This may be difficult at first, but the point is to train yourself to relate to chords, strums, and lyrics in a variety of ways so that when you encounter them outside the realm of this book, you'll be prepared. Remember to keep the strum pattern even and in time. I've only included the strum on the first extra verse and the chords on the first and second. See if you can make the leap from the printed music to the lyrics only below. (This will not go on your permanent record.) By the way, this single down strum is quite elementary but you'll still hear it a lot in pop music. I just noticed it on Elvis' *Burning Love*. Flash: I just heard *Handsome Molly* on the radio—by Mike Jagger on his CD **Wandering Spirit.** Don't that beat all!!!

Handsome Molly

Traditional - Key of A

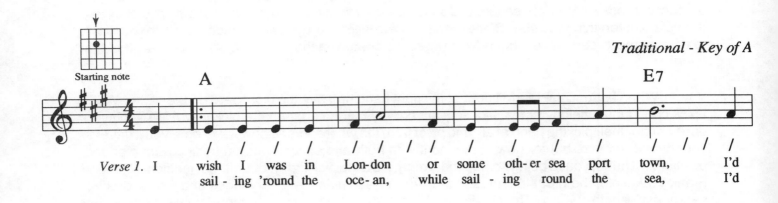

Verse 1. I wish I was in Lon-don or some oth-er sea port town, I'd
sail-ing 'round the oce-an, while sail-ing round the sea, I'd

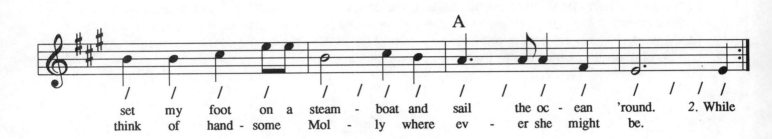

set my foot on a steam-boat and sail the oce-an 'round. 2. While
think of hand-some Mol-ly where ev-er she might be.

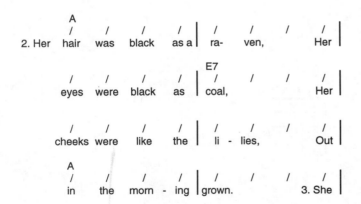

2. Her hair was black as a | ra-ven, Her
eyes were black as | coal, Her
cheeks were like the | li-lies, Out
in the morn-ing | grown. 3. She

A
rode to church on Sunday,
E7
She passed me on by,

I saw her mind was changing
A
By the roving of her eye.

4. Don't you remember Molly,
When you gave me your right hand?
You said if ever you'd marry,
That I would be your man.

5. Now you've broken your promise,
Go home with who you please,
While my poor heart is aching
You're lying at your ease.

MINIMUM MUSIC THEORY

Here's a tiny bit of music theory. The first two songs we learned were written in 4/4 ("four four") or common time. Look in the upper left-hand corner of the music and you'll see what's called the time signature. C (for common time) and 4/4 are interchangeable. The top 4 tells us that we've divided the song into measures with four beats in them. The bottom 4 tells us that a quarter note gets one beat. If we counted the feel of the song we'd say "One - two - three - four, One - two - three - four," etc. *I Ride an Old Paint* is in 3/4 or waltz time. In 3/4, the 3 tells us that the song is divided into measures with three beats in them. The 4 tells us that a quarter note gets one beat. If we counted the feel of this song we'd say "One - two - three, One - two - three," etc. These are the two most common time signatures in country music, though you may hear or see 2/4 or 6/8. For our purposes, we'll think of them as variations on 4/4 and 3/4.

I RIDE AN OLD PAINT, C & G7 CHORDS

Old Paint has more new chords, C and G7, and the changes come a little quicker. To complicate things further, let's add two new strums! And don't forget your flatpick! (As you'll see, *Old Paint* has a Western theme. Now you're proficient in <u>both</u> types of music, country **and** Western.)

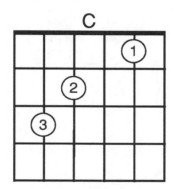 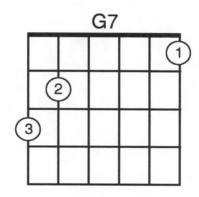

The first new strum is almost identical to the last, except instead of four strums to the measure, we'll play only three — "down - down - down." The second strum will be "down – down– down-up." You'll have to fit the "down-up" into the same space the single down strums fit into, and the count of the song will still be the basic "one – two – three, one – two – three," etc. However, the strum will be counted like this: "one – two – three and, one – two – three and" to accommodate the up strum. We'll use this little tent character (∧) to represent the down-up strum.

Strum: /   /   ∧
        down   down   down-up
          1   2   3-and

These strums are demonstrated on the tape. Practice both on the exercise below before you try the song. You may find the up strum a little difficult to control at first. You don't have to hit all six strings on the up strum. In fact, most players only hit the first three or four strings. Once you can change the chords smoothly and play either strum at will (or Dave or Bill), alternate strums on different verses. Kathy Mattea uses a basic down strum pattern with some up strokes thrown in from time to time on *What Could Have Been*.

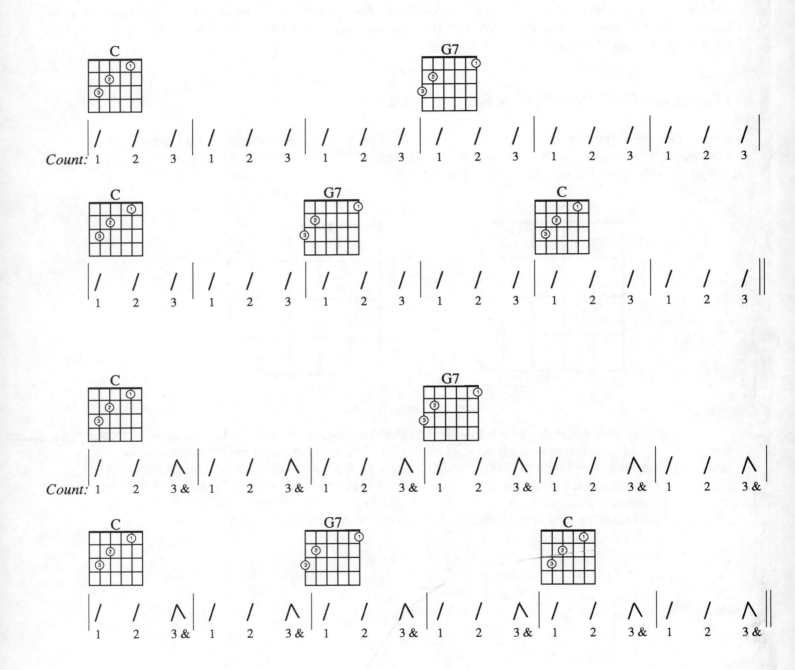

I Ride an Old Paint

Counter #: _____

Traditional - Key of C

1. I ride an old paint, I lead an old Dan, I'm going to Mon-tan-a to
2. Old Bill Jones had a daugh-ter and a son, One went to Den-ver the

throw a Hool-i-an. They feed 'em in the cool-ies they wa-ter in the
oth-er we-nt wrong. His wife she died in a pool room

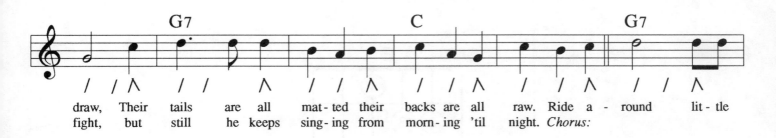

draw, Their tails are all mat-ted their backs are all raw. Ride a-round lit-tle
fight, but still he keeps sing-ing from morn-ing 'til night. *Chorus:*

doggies ride arou-nd re-al slow for the fier-y and the snuf-fy are rar-ing to go.

         C
3. When I die, take my saddle from the wall,
G7   C
Put it on my pony and lead him from the stall.
      G7   C
Tie my bones to his back, turn our faces to the
west
      G7   C
And we'll ride the prairie that we love the best.

(Chorus)

RED RIVER VALLEY

I'm sure you know our next song. If I'm wrong, then I'll be a dirty sidewinder. *Red River Valley* is a great old country tune, one of the absolute all-time standards. The new chords are E and B7, and you'll have somewhat of a choice as to when you play them. By that I mean that the B7 and E7, some of which are marked with parentheses in the music, are optional the first few times you work through the song. As soon as you feel comfortable without them, put them in! The song will sound more interesting with the extra chords. This strum is even more exotic than the last: / / ∧ ∧ or "down, down, down-up, down-up." This strum is counted "one - two - three and - four and, one-two-three and-four and."

```
   /      /      ∧        ∧
"down, down, down-up, down-up."
1      2      3 and    4 and
```

In place of the new chord/strum exercises you've used up to this point, try making an exercise out of the music as written. Work through it slowly, concentrating on the chord changes and keeping the strums even.

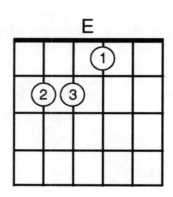

E

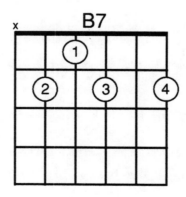

B7

24

Red River Valley

Traditional - Key of E

Starting note

Verse 1. From this val - ley they say you are go - ing. We will
sit by my side if you love me. Do not

miss your bright eyes and sweet smile. For they
has - ten to bid me a - dieu. Just re -

say you are tak - ing the sun - shine, That has
mem - ber the Red Riv - er Val - ley, And the

bright - ened our path - ways a - while. *Chorus:* Come and
cow - boy who loved you so true.

2. Won't you think of the | val - ley you're | leaving?
Oh how | lone- ly, how | sad it will |
be. Oh think | of the fond |
heart you are | breaking, And the |
grief you are | caus - ing to | me. Come and |

3. As you go to your home by the ocean,
May you never forget those sweet hours,
That we spent in the Red River Valley,
And the love we exchanged 'mid the flowers.

25

MINOR CHORDS, SHADY GROVE

About now you're probably thinking, "Isn't it time we learned some minor chords?" Yes! Minor chords are denoted by a lower case "m" following a letter name as in Em or Am, which we say as "E minor" and "A minor." Minor chords have one different note from the basic triads. We won't get too deeply into the music theory behind it, but here's what it all amounts to. When you play an A chord, you're sounding the notes A (fifth string open and third string second fret), C♯ (second string second fret), and E (sixth string open, fourth string second fret, and first string open). (C♯ is pronounced "C-sharp.") These notes are the first (A), the third (C♯), and the fifth (E) notes of the A major scale:

A	B	C♯	D	E	F♯	G♯	A
do	re	me	fa	sol	la	ti	do
1	2	3	4	5	6	7	8

When you play an Am chord you're sounding the notes A (fifth string open and third string second fret), C natural (second string first fret), and E (sixth string open, fourth string second fret, and first string open). (C without a sharp sign is "C natural" or just plain C.) So, if you take a major triad, like the A chord, and lower what's called the third of the chord, (in this case C♯), one half step to C, you end up with an Am chord!

Just for the sake of confusion, let's look at the A7 chord. When you play an A7 chord, you're sounding four different notes instead of the three of the triad (*tri* means three): A (fifth string open), C♯ (second string second fret), E (sixth string open, fourth string second fret, and first string open), and G natural (third string open). The first three notes are the same as the regular A-chord triad, but then we add a G note. I sense a puzzled look on your face, and knowing that your mama didn't raise no fools, I'll continue. No doubt you remember that the notes of the A-major scale are A, B, C♯, D, E, F♯, G♯. Therein lies the rub: the seventh note of the A-major scale is a G♯, not a G natural, as I just said was in the A7 chord. It's kind of a dirty trick, but dominant seventh chords, like A7, E7, G7, B♭7, F7, etc., use the *flatted* seventh note of the scale. In this case we see that the seventh note of the A-major scale is a G♯ note. We lower it one half step to G natural, slap it on the A triad and poof, we have an A7 chord.

OK, back to minor chords. The following song, the great American country classic *Shady Grove*, is presented in two different keys, E-minor modal and A minor modal. This will give you practice on two different minor chords, and also help you get used to the idea that you can sing and play a song in more than one key. The E-minor version pretty well fits with my voice, but may be too low or high for you. The A-minor version might be perfect for you, but a little high for me. Later in the book we'll discuss this transposition process more. You'll have a quick chord change in the last two measures (from Em to D and back to Em in the first version, Am to G back to Am in the second version) where each chord gets two beats. Work on this as much as you need to, to be able to make the changes smoothly without slowing down. (Of course, there is an easy way out: stay on the D or G chord from the previous measure. However, if you take the easy way, you'll never learn about fast changes.) The strum for *Shady Grove* is / ∧ / ∧ or "down, down-up, down, down-up."

```
    /      ∧      /      ∧
"down, down-up, down, down-up."
    1    2 and    3    4 and
```

Practice it and the new chord on each song before you try singing along with the tape. Merle Haggard uses a similar strum on his classic, *Silver Wings.* Here are the new chords:

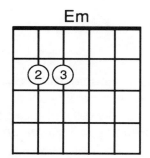
Em

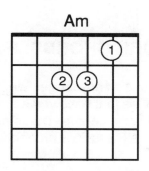
Am

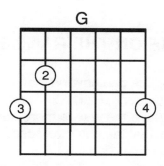
G

By now the flatpick should be feeling pretty comfortable in your hand. If not, take some time to concentrate on working with it. You'll need it!

Shady Grove - E minor modal

Counter #: _____

Traditional - Key of Em modal

Starting note

| Em | D | Em |

Verse 1. Cheeks as red as the bloom ing rose, Eyes of the deep - est brown, You
Chorus: Sha - dy Grove, my little love, Sha - dy Grove I say,

| D | Em | D | Em |

are the dar - ling of my heart, Stay till the sun goes down.
Sha - dy Grove, my lit - tle love, I'm bound to go a - way.

Shady Grove - A minor modal

Counter #: _____

Traditional - Key of Am modal

Starting note

| Am | G | Am |

Verse 1. Peach - es in the Sum - mer - time, App - les in the Fall, If
Verse 2. Sha - dy Grove, my little love, Stand - ing in the door,

| G | Am | G | Am |

I can't have my pretty lit - tle miss, I'll have no one at all.
Shoes and stock - ings in her hand, Little bare feet on the floor.

27

HOME ON THE RANGE, TOUGH CHORDS: F and B♭

The bad news is that we can't put it off any longer, we have to learn a couple of chords that are very tough: F and B♭. The good news is that once you learn them, they're incredibly useful and they'll pave the way to more advanced barre chords. That didn't hurt a bit, now did it? More good news is that the song we'll use to learn the F and B♭ is probably quite familiar to you— *Home on the Range*.

The chord diagram for the F has two circled #1s. This does not mean that you need to have two index fingers to play the chord, rather that you use your index finger to play both the first and second strings at the first fret. (This is sometimes denoted in chord grids with one oval covering the strings and frets.) It will take some time to get this to sound clear — you'll have to build up those index finger muscles. Probably the most difficult part of playing the B♭ chord is that you have to avoid strumming the first and sixth strings. (Notice the small "x" above these strings.) I try to damp the first string with the part of my first finger closest to the first string, and avoid playing the sixth with my picking hand. The song is a waltz, in 3/4, just like *Old Paint*, and we'll use a new strum. This time try:

```
   /       ∧       ∧
"down, down-up, down-up."
   1     2 and    3 and
```

As you work through the different songs and strums, you're bound to find favorites. While that's fun, don't let it keep you from discovering new strums, and experiment with swapping the strums around from song to song. For example, the "down, down, down-up" strum from *Old Paint* will work just fine here and vice versa. And, as you play, you're bound to make changes and create new strums of your own. Have at it!

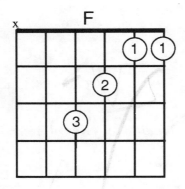

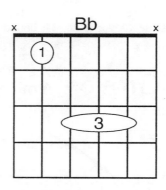

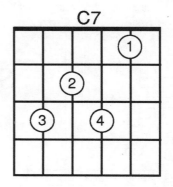

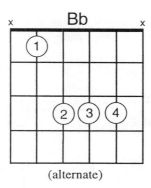

(alternate)

28

Home on the Range

Traditional - Key of F

Verse 1. Oh give me a home, Where the buff - a - lo roam, Where the deer and the
Verse 2. Oh give me the land where the bright dia - mond sand, Throws its light from the

ant - e - lope play, Where sel - dom is heard, a dis - cour - a - ging
glit - ter - ing streams, Where glid - eth a - long the grace - ful white

word, And the skies are not clou - dy all day. *Chorus:* Home,
swan, Like the maid to her heav - en - ly dreams.

home on the range, Where the deer and the ant - e - lope play,

Where sel - dom is heard, a dis - cour - a - ging word, And the

skies are not clou - dy all day.

3. Where the air is so pure, the zephyrs so free, The
breezes so balmy and light. That I
would not ex - change my home on the range, For
all of the cit - ies so bright.

29

GOING DOWN THIS ROAD FEELING BAD

Going Down This Road Feeling Bad is a favorite song of mine. It shows up in all kinds of country styles, from old time and bluegrass to modern honky-tonk country. The strum is a sprightly / ∧∧∧ or "down, down-up, down-up, down-up" and (counted "one - two and - three and - four and") that will lead us into a whole new set of accompaniment patterns, where we pick a bass note and then strum a chord. Extra verses are below. *Going Down This Road Feeling Bad* is another one that cries out for you to add your own verses. You know, life on the road can be pretty dismal — travelling from town to town with a bunch of musicians who don't believe in changing their socks. I've added the verses, "No deli platter in the dressing room" and "Can't find my pick with both hands," etc.

The song itself starts out on a G chord and moves on to a C. Notice the G7 chord between the two. The G7 (called a *dominant seven* chord), is a transition chord from G to C, and you can use it in any similar cases, like in the eighth measure. This holds true for the same type of chordal motion in any other key. For example, if you're in the key of E, playing an E chord and moving to an A chord, the E7 will lead you from the E to the A. Same with C — C7 — F, A — A7 — D, F — F7 — B♭, etc. We'll talk more about chords and keys later on. In the meantime, look back over the songs you've already learned and see if you can find places to add transitional dominant seven chords.

<table>
<tr><td>G</td><td></td><td>G7</td></tr>
</table>

3. They feed me on corn bread and beans,
    C   G
They feed me on corn bread and beans,
    C   G   Em
They feed me on corn bread and beans,
    G   D7   G
And I ain't gonna be treated this a way.

4. I'm going where the chilly winds don't blow etc.
5. I'm going where the water tastes like wine, etc.
6. I'm going where the weather suits my clothes, etc.

30

THE CUCKOO

The Cuckoo is another special favorite that I recorded for my **Folk Heart** record. It's another minor-sounding song to teach you the Dm chord. The strum is / / ∧ / or "down, down, down-up, down" counted "one - two - three and - four."

Dm

The Cuckoo

Counter #: _____

Traditional - Key of Dm modal

Starting note

Dm

Verse 1. Oh the cuck - oo, she's a pretty bird, And she
Dia - monds, Jack of dia - monds, I –

C   Am   Dm

war - bles as she flies. And she
know you of – old. You –

nev - er, says "cuck - oo," 'till the
robbed my poor pock - ets, of my

C   Am   Dm

fourth day, of Ju - ly. Verse 2. Jack of
sil - ver and my gold.

Dm
3. I've played cards in England
   C   Am Dm
I've played cards in Spain.

I'll bet you ten dollars
   C   Am Dm
I'll beat you next game.

4. My horses ain't hungry
They won't eat your hay.
I'll drive on a little further
I'll feed them on the way.

31

I GET BLUE

I wrote two songs especially for this book, just for you, and this is the first. (The second is *Nobody Sleeps at My House*. The others by me are from my solid-gold archives.)

As you know, this book is mainly about playing rhythm guitar. To really understand the role that rhythm guitar plays in modern country music, you need to listen very carefully. Rhythm guitar is always an important part of the sound, though it is subtle and more in the background than other elements like voice, lead lines, etc. (Never say the following on a gig or at a recording session: "If she'd quit singing so damn loud, I could hear my guitar.") In preparation for putting this book together, I grabbed a cross-section of country artists' CDs and listened to them on headphones. It was rare to find one without at least one acoustic rhythm guitar, some had three, all playing different though complementary parts. Listen again to your favorite recordings, use headphones if you can, and try to tune out everything but the rhythm guitar until you identify the strum or pattern. Then listen again and determine how that rhythm guitar part fits with the rest of the ensemble. Next, try learning the pattern and applying it to the songs you know. You'll find that there's a vast range of slightly different rhythm guitar styles that you can change and fit to just about any musical situation. You'll also hear that the same strum given different accents can change the feel of a pattern any number of ways. Records by The Judds and the O'Kanes are rich with audible acoustic rhythm guitar.

The strum for *I Get Blue* is constant down-up strums: ∧ ∧ ∧ ∧ or "down-up, down-up, down-up, down-up," counted "one and - two and - three and - four and." This strum, and variations of it, seem to be the most popular in current country. Billy Ray Cyrus' *Achy Breaky Heart* has it, Randy Travis' *On the Other Hand*, George Jones' *The Race is One*, Buck Owens' *Together Again*, George Strait's *A Fire I Can't Put Out*, behind the chorus to Vern Gosdin's *Do You Believe Me Now?*, Patty Loveless' *Can't Stop Myself From Loving You*, Garth Brooks' *That Summer*, Merle Haggard's *Misery & Gin*, and The Desert Rose Band's *One Step Forward*, all use a variation of it. Even the Beatles' *Yellow Submarine* has a strum like this. *Queen of Hearts* by Juice Newton uses a variation: ∨∧∧∧ ("rest-up, down-up, down-up, down-up" "rest-and, two-and, three-and, four-and") as a fill. Rodney Crowell combines it with "down, down-up, down-up, down-up" on *'Til I Gain Control Again.* From the range of songs I listed, you can see how versatile this strum is.

I Get Blue

by Dix Bruce - Key of C

Chorus: I get blue, All on ac - count of you.
new at love, Not in the Cheat - in' Club.

And the way you do, You make me blue.
Or in the Ly in' League, Now won't you tell me please.

You make me cry, I got blood - shot eyes,
And tell me true, What did you do,

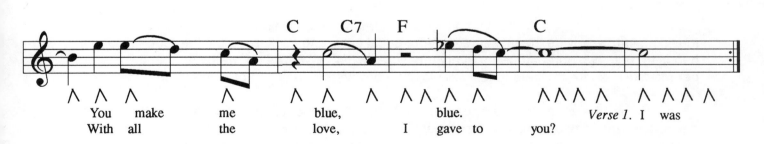

You make me blue, blue.
With all the love, I gave to you? *Verse 1.* I was

```
        G7              C
2. Beginner's luck don't count for much
        G7              C
When you're in love with a skunk
        F             G7
Or a dirty dog who runs a-round
               C   C7   F
Wasting your love
        C
All over town.
```

3. Now I learned to cheat
And how to lie
How to sneak around
And make somebody cry
Make somebody blue
When I'm not true
All the world can thank
Nobody but you!

GET SOME SONGBOOKS!

By now you've played most of the typical easy guitar chords: triads, dominant sevens, and minors, and you've learned several strums as well. It's very important now to play, play, and play them, to the point that they are second nature to your head and fingers. If you aren't playing from songbooks of your favorite country stars now, you need to do it soon. In fact, jump in the pickup right now and get down to your local music store and buy a book or two. (You'll get the most mileage out of a "Top Hits" "Country Classics" -type book with lots of different artists represented.) Most songbooks include chord diagrams and all should have chord letters. If the songbook doesn't at least have chord letter designations, jump back in the pickup and forget the whole thing until you find a songbook that does. If you know chord names but need chord diagrams, look them up in the Chord Dictionary at the back of this book. Challenge yourself to find new songs to play, and exercise your knowledge of chords and strums. Get together with friends who sing and play, and jam with them. Keep that music running through your head and hands as much as possible. The more you do it, the easier it will become and the more fun you'll have. (Did I mention how important it is to play?) Sheet music will probably not be an exact representation of a recording. It may not even be written in the same key as the recording you're used to hearing, and won't sound right if you play along. However, with a little practice at transposing (moving the chords and melody to a different key), or help from a more advanced player, you'll probably be able to find something that works. The process of trying will teach you tons.

ALTERNATING BASS NOTE – STRUM TECHNIQUE

Next up is an exploration of the mother of all country accompaniment, the alternating bass note – strum technique. In this technique, we pick a bass note and then strum a chord immediately after. The effect is that your accompaniment supplies both a bass line and a rhythm strum. It's most noticeable in bluegrass and old time music, but also popular in country music: Dwight Yoakam's *The Distance Between You and Me*, George Jones' *She Thinks I Still Care* (aka *She Stinks I Smell Fair*), with bass notes and down-up strums, Paulette Carlson with *Highway 101* ditto on *Whiskey, If You Were a Woman*. As we work on the bass note – strum technique, we'll identify the bass notes in all of the most common chords so that you'll eventually be able to use this technique on any song in the repertoire.

As you know, 4/4, and 3/4 are the most common meters or time signatures found in country music. In 4/4, we divide the measure into four equal parts and think, sing, tap our foot, or clap our hands to "one, two, three, four" for every measure. In 3/4, or waltz time, we have "one, two, three" per measure, and with these tunes you played a down strum on each of these three beats.

Within the measure we separate beats into "downbeats" and "backbeats." In 4/4, the downbeats are on beats one and three, backbeats are on two and four. In 3/4, the downbeat is on beat one, backbeats are on two and three. The diagram below illustrates this with beat numbers, downbeats and backbeats.

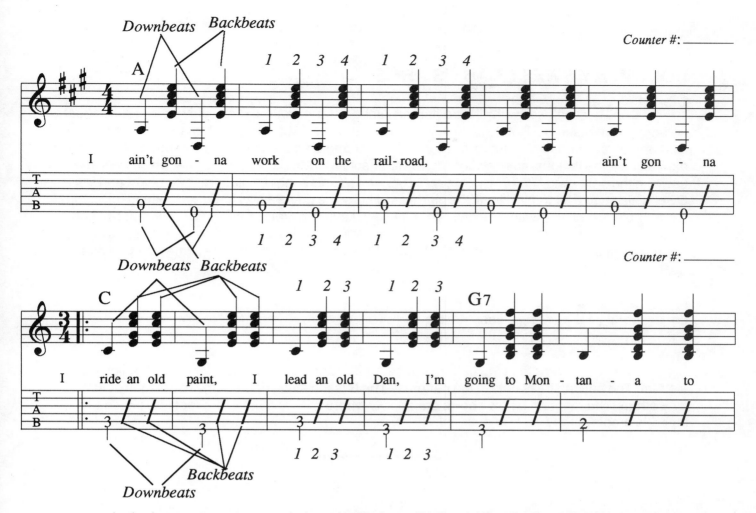

In the bass note – strum technique (we'll also call it flatpick backup) we pick a bass note on each downbeat and strum a chord on each backbeat. The backbeats give the whole measure its "groove," so don't be shy about playing them out. The ultimate effect of this punch on the backbeats is a kind of "one, TWO, three, FOUR" in 4/4 feel, and "one TWO, THREE, one, TWO, THREE" in 3/4.

In flatpick backup, the "root tone" or "one" of the chord is always played on the first downbeat. (In the case of an A chord, this will be an A bass note, fifth string open.) "Root" and "one" are interchangeable terms, and always have the same name as the chord. (For example, the root of the Bb chord is a Bb note, the root of the E chord is an E note, etc.) The root is followed by a strum (or two strums if you are in 3/4). The next downbeat is most often the "five" of whatever chord you are playing, but can also be the "three," as with the G chord (fifth string second fret B note) or the C chord (fourth string second fret E note). This is again followed by a strum or strums. In 3/4 our second bass note, the "five" or "three" of the chord, will be on the first beat of the next measure followed again by two strums. This is often referred to as playing "alternating bass." The pattern that describes what we're doing is "root, strum, five, strum" for a song in 4/4, and "root, strum, strum, five, strum, strum" for a song in 3/4 or waltz time. The pattern is one measure in length for 4/4 and two measures in length for 3/4.

4/4 Measure Count	1	2	3	4		
Chord part	root	strum	five	strum		

3/4 Measure Count	1	2	3	1	2	3
Chord part	root	strum	strum	five	strum	strum

ROLL IN MY SWEET BABY'S ARMS

Don't get confused with all the different numbers flying around. Previously we discussed beat numbers in measures. "Root" (or "one"), "three," and "five" refer to notes in scales and chords. Remember that a chord is three or more notes strummed simultaneously, and that chords are derived from the various major scales (do-re-mi-fa-sol-la-ti-do). Here's the A scale, which we'll make use of in the next song, *Roll In My Sweet Baby's Arms.* (This song is a bluegrass standard and Buck Owens also had a hit with it. I think the plot is as follows: the guy is a lazy good-for-nothing {probably a banjo player} whose wife or significant other works in a bakery. She comes home from work, hungry, he sees her at the door with her bundle and thinks, "There's a roll in my sweet baby's arms," since she usually gets to take home day-old baked goods.) The 1 and 8 are the same note one *octave* apart.

A	B	C♯	D	E	F♯	G♯	A
do	re	mi	fa	sol	la	ti	do
1	2	3	4	5	6	7	8

The first bass note in the pattern will be A (fifth string open — the root or one), followed by a strum. The second bass note in the pattern will be E (sixth string open — the five), again followed by a strum. The diagram below shows graphically where the bass notes are located. Listen to the taped example.

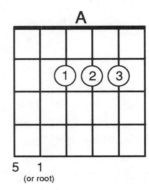

We also need to determine the bass notes for the other two chords in *Roll in My Sweet Baby's Arms,* the D and E7, so we have to look at the major scales for each of them.

D	E	F♯	G	A	B	C♯	D
do	re	mi	fa	sol	la	ti	do
1	2	3	4	5	6	7	8

E	F♯	G♯	A	B	C♯	D♯	E
do	re	mi	fa	sol	la	ti	do
1	2	3	4	5	6	7	8

These major scales tell us that the one or root of D is D, the five is A; the root of E is E, the five is B. The diagrams on the next page show us where these bass notes are: the one of D is the fourth string open, the five is the fifth string open; the root of E7 is the sixth string open, the five is on the fifth string second fret. The Chord Dictionary at the back of the book identifies where the bass notes are for the most common chords. It also shows which part of the chord (1, 3, 5, 7, flat 3, etc.) each string supplies. The Scale and Transposition Chart (page 67) shows all of the major scales.

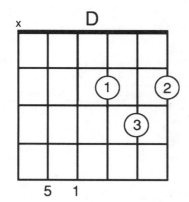 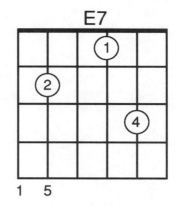

As always, practice the pattern (shown on the music where strums have been up to this point — R = root, St = strum, 5 = um, er, well 5!), with the chords, and don't play any faster than you can change the chords cleanly and without stopping before you play *Roll In My Sweet Baby's Arms.*

Here's the pattern again:

4/4 Measure Count	1	2	3	4
Chord part	R	St	5	St

You'll have to memorize which notes go with which chords. The bass notes for A7, which you'll need in the tenth full measure, are the same as for the A triad. This is almost always the case with different types of chords with the same letter name. That's very good news as you'll really only have to learn two bass notes to play over three types of chords: major, seventh and minor. Use the exercise below to practice the bass/strum moves on the chords. This exercise should be used on the next several songs to learn the new patterns by chord. Rodney Crowell uses similar patterns on *Leavin' Louisiana:* "Root, down, down, down" and "Root, down, down–up, down." Check out Buck Owen's oldie *I've Got a Tiger by the Tail* with its "Root, down–up, down–up, down–up."

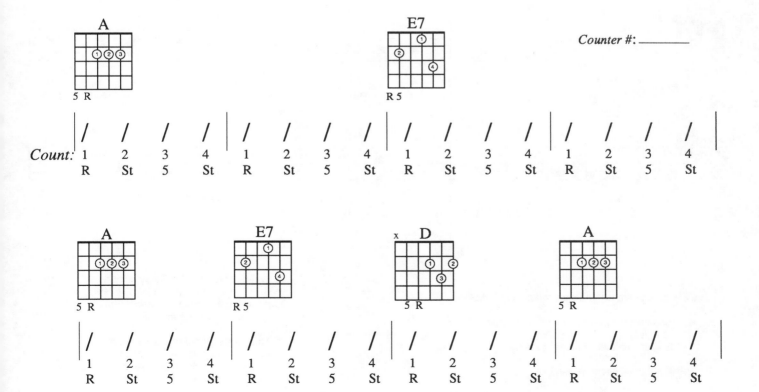

37

Roll In My Sweet Baby's Arms

Counter #: _____

Traditional - Key of A

Verse 1. I ain't gon - na work on the rail-road, I ain't gon - na

Verse 2. Some - times there's a change in the wea-ther, Some - times there's a

work on the farm, I'll lay a- round the shack 'till the mail train gets

change in the sea, Some - times there's a change in my own true

back, And I'll roll in my sweet ba - by's arms.

love, But there's nev - er a change in me.

Chorus: Roll in my sweet ba- by's arms, Roll in my sweet ba- by's

arms, Lay a- round the shack 'till the mail train gets

back, And I'll roll in my sweet ba - by's arms.

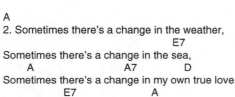

A
2. Sometimes there's a change in the weather,
                                 E7
Sometimes there's a change in the sea,
    A   A7   D
Sometimes there's a change in my own true love,
        E7   A
But there's never a change in me.

3. Where were you last Friday night,
While I was lying in jail?
Out walking the street with another man,
You wouldn't even go my bail.

4. They say your parents don't like me,
They drove me away from your door,
If I had my life to live over again,
I'd never go there any more.

The beauty of this pattern is that it can be one of the most useful and applicable things you'll learn in the country style. It can be expanded with connecting runs (we'll get into those next) and modified into a lead technique known generically as Carter picking after Mother Maybelle Carter of the Original Carter Family. The basic backup technique that you are perfecting now is, by itself, especially helpful in smaller acoustic situations where the guitarist is responsible for playing the bass line *and* the backbeat, as in bluegrass, old timey, or more traditionally oriented country groups.

Once you can play *Roll in My Sweet Baby's Arms,* take some time to go back over the songs in the beginning of this book, or any other songs you know, and work them out with flatpick backup. Play along with the taped versions of the songs this time adjusting the balance of your stereo to hear the flatpick backup. Start with *My Home's Across the Blue Ridge Mountains* and *Handsome Molly.* You'll find the chords diagrammed in the back of the book.

While you practice and memorize each chord and its bass notes, remember that strums will not necessarily include all six strings. If you've picked a bass note on the sixth string, your strum will generally be on strings five or four through one. You won't play the sixth string again as part of your strum, but you will let the bass note ring with the following strum. If you pick a bass note on the fourth string, your strum will be on strings three through one and so on. There are no requirements, and you'll discover that you can achieve different rhythmic effects by strumming more or less strings.

CONNECTING RUNS, TABLATURE

Let's add a bit of spice to our basic flatpick backup with some connecting runs. The music that follows will show you a whole chorus of backup written out. To do this, we'll need to learn about *tablature.*

Tablature is an alternative to standard music notation. We use it in teaching as a shortcut to music reading. Rather than reading notes, the player reads positions. Numbers are arranged on a six-line staff with each line representing one of the strings on the guitar. The top line of the tablature staff represents the first string (E and highest pitched) of the guitar, second from the top is the second string (B), third from the top is the third string (G), etc., on down to the bottom line which represents the sixth-string low E. (This is the famous "bottom line" that people are always talking about.) Numbers on these lines represent fret numbers on the different strings. So, if the top line has the numbers 5, 4, 3, 2, 1 left to right, you should play the note on the fifth fret of the first string followed by the note at the fourth fret of the first string, then the third, second, and first frets, in succession. Stems and circles around these numbers tell how long to hold each note and define the rhythm of the melody.

Tablature Staff

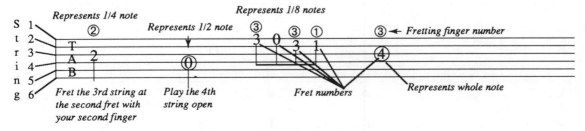

Guitar Fingerboard

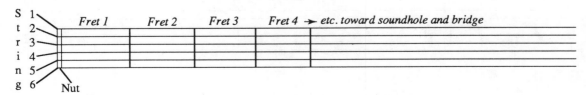

These tab symbols have the same time value as the standard notes on which they're based, so ultimately, you need to understand a little about the rhythm of standard music notation to make the connection. In 4/4, a whole note = four counts, half note = 2 counts, quarter note = 1 count, eighth note = 1/2 count (or two eighth notes = one count). To play a whole note, you'd pick it and let it ring over the duration of counting from one to four in your head, and etc. for the other notes. / = single down strums, just like you've seen in the strum sections, ∧ = a down-up strum. In most cases, each of these will equal one beat in the measure. Circled numbers above the staff indicate which fretting fingers to use.

BURY ME BENEATH THE WILLOW, BASS NOTE CONNECTORS

Here's the melody to *Bury Me Beneath the Willow*. Below the lyrics the flatpick accompaniment is shown in tablature. Be sure to listen to the tape before you try playing it. Pay close attention to the circled numbers <u>above</u> the tab staff and remember that these tell you which fretting fingers to use to play the connecting runs. Obviously, you can use any of your four fingers (and often the thumb) to play any note of the fingerboard. The trick is to hold the basic chord position and use the finger that's closest to the new fret you need to cover. That way you can cleanly and easily slip in and out of position without wasting motion, time, and energy. As you advance, you'll use the best finger automatically as a matter of course, so it's important to get started correctly now.

Bury Me Beneath the Willow

Counter #: _____

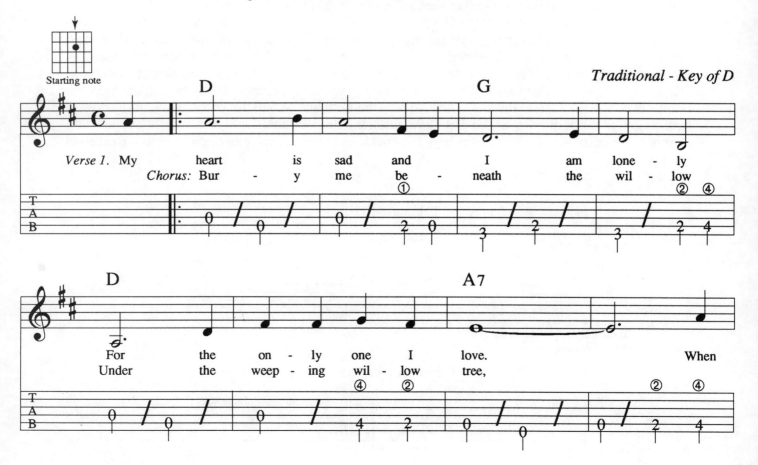

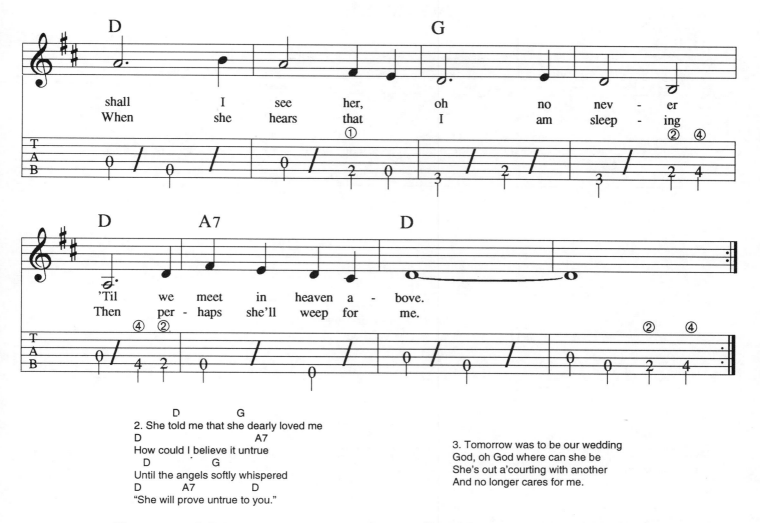

2. She told me that she dearly loved me
D A7
How could I believe it untrue
D G
Until the angels softly whispered
D A7 D
"She will prove untrue to you."

3. Tomorrow was to be our wedding
God, oh God where can she be
She's out a'courting with another
And no longer cares for me.

There are an infinite number of ways to connect different chords. The connecting runs shown in *Bury Me Beneath the Willow* are quite simple and should be memorized generically. For example, the last half of measure two connects a D chord to a G chord. **This connector can be used anywhere you have a D chord moving to a G chord.** You may have to change it slightly as in the case of a waltz or a song in a key other then D, but basically it will work wherever a chord progression moves from D to G. You can also change these runs according to your own taste. As you listen to and play this style of music, changes will naturally occur to you. Try to find different ways to play these runs, and other runs you hear live or on a record, and work on inventing your own. Measure six has a run moving from a D chord to an A7. Again, this can be used anywhere you find these chord changes. In measure eight, the run is inverted as the chord progression moves from A7 back to D. In most cases, connecting runs will work in the opposite direction. *My Home's Across the Blue Ridge Mountains* had two chords, the D and the A7. Play through it again and add the connecting runs from *Bury Me Beneath the Willow.*

SOME DRINK

Some Drink is a similar exercise in a different key (G) and different meter (3/4). Listen to it on the tape. Measure three has a connector from a G to a C chord. I didn't reverse it to move back down to the G in the fourth measure, but one certainly could. Measure sixteen connects a G chord with a D7. Memorize these but start working on your own runs as well. It's time to try double strums ("down-up" ∧) in flatpick backup. They work just like they did with straight strums, you substitute a "down-up" strum (noted by this symbol ∧ and count "one and two and" etc.) for a single down strum. Up strums are usually played on only the first two or three strings. Once you have a handle on these connectors, try them on *Going Down This Road Feeling Bad.* As you practice all these new and wonderful things, spend most of your time working on the parts that give you trouble, not the things that come easily!

Some Drink

Counter #: _____

by Dix Bruce - Key of G

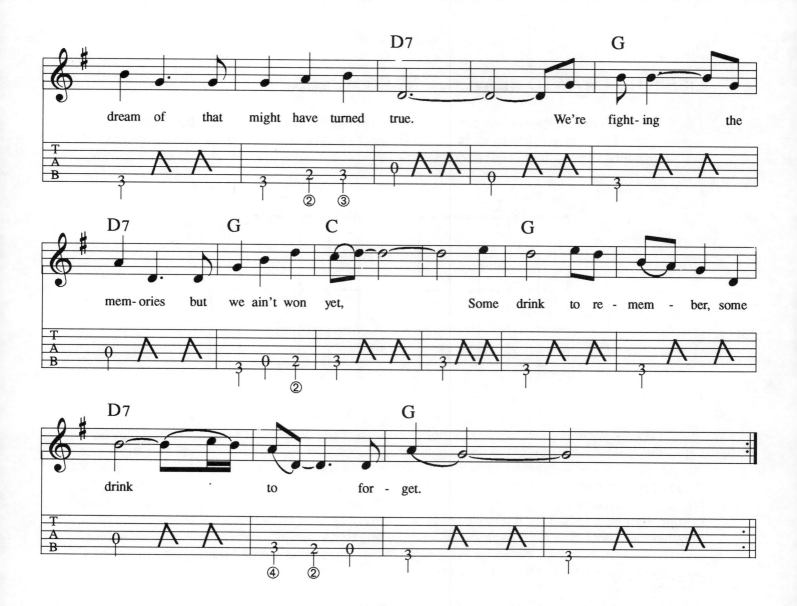

3. Thomas was an outlaw, a wild young man

G   D7   G   C

He looks back through his whiskey, far back as he can

But he still sees the young man that hasn't lost yet

Some drink to remember, some drink to forget.

4. John's pouring drinks, he does everyday,

He never asks questions, knows what not to say.

We say, "Set 'em up," and he says, "You bet!"

Some drink to remember, some drink to forget.

5. Me, I just come here for the talk and the jokes,

I'm not really hurting like these other folks,

But sometimes at bartime my eyes feel wet,

Some drink to remember, some drink to forget.

LIFE'S RAILWAY TO HEAVEN, FINGER MOVES

Up until now, all the bass notes we've played in the flatpick backup have been a part of the regular chords held to play the song. In *Life's Railway to Heaven* we'll need to move a finger to fret the alternate bass note, in this case the five of each chord, on the C and F chords shown below.

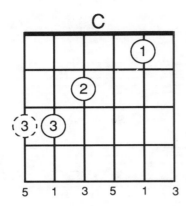
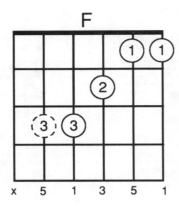

These diagrams look similar to those you've already seen. You'll recall that the numbers below the grid tell what part of the chord each string supplies. The dotted circle indicates the finger that needs to move and the fret it needs to be moved to. In both the C and F you'll be lifting up your third finger from one string, and moving it over to another to get the other bass note. Practice playing the bass/strum pattern and moving your third finger. These moves are noted in the tablature. Be sure to keep your fretting hand in the basic position of the chord. Don't release the chord to grab a bass or connecting note unless you absolutely have to. Any unnecessary hand motion will work against you. (This is one of the few instances in your life when laziness and sloth will be rewarded.) The trick is to smoothly integrate notes with strums.

Life's Railway also has bass connectors between the chords. Again you should memorize them as they'll work anywhere you find the same chord moves: C to F, F to C, C to D7, D7 to G7, G7 to C. All can be reversed. One thing we have to guard against is playing too many connectors, and you'll find that in a few places I've left them out. Use your own judgment as to where to place them, remembering that you don't have to always use the runs. Simple bass notes and strums can often be the most effective.

In measures 31, 33, 37, and 40, I've added alternate bass notes on several chords. In flatpick backup we usually play the "root, strum, five, strum" pattern. However, we can substitute the three for the five for variety's sake. While any note in a chord can be used, I suggest sticking to the 1, 3, or 5 and using the lowest pitched note possible.

The last measure of the chorus shows a connector that doesn't connect to anything. It's meant to lead you back to the top of the music and the second verse. You can also use this as a lead in at the very beginning of a song.

Once you can play *Life's Railway* comfortably, lift the connectors and patterns and apply them to *Old Paint* and *Some Drink*. Keep in mind that you will have to convert the bass/strum pattern from one measure ("root, strum, five, strum") to a two-measure pattern ("root, strum, strum, five, strum, strum").

Life's Railway to Heaven

Traditional - Key of C

rail.   *Chorus:* Bless- ed   sav —   ior thou wilt   guide us,   'Till we

(alt. bass note)   *(alt. bass note)*   ② *(finger move)*   ③ *(finger move)*   *(alt. bass note)*

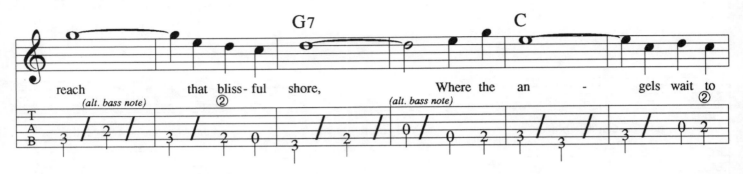

reach   that bliss- ful   shore,   Where the   an —   gels wait to

(alt. bass note)   ②   *(alt. bass note)*   ②

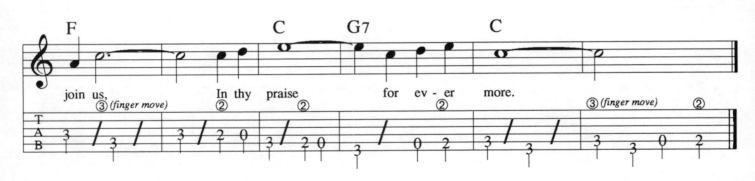

join us,   In thy   praise   for   ev - er   more.

③ *(finger move)*   ②   ②   ②   ③ *(finger move)*   ②

THE CAPO

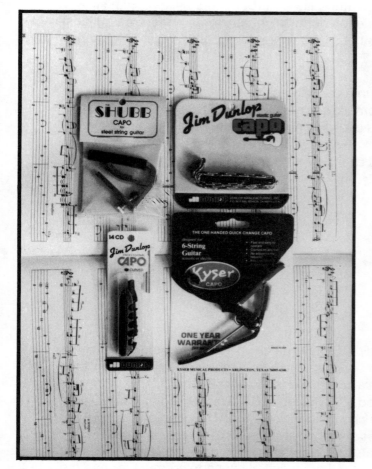

Capos courtesy of the 5th string, Berkeley

Shubb brand capo on 2nd fret

A capo is a clamp that can be positioned on the guitar neck to effectively "shorten" the length of the strings. We place the capo in any fret slightly behind the metal fretwire, adjust it until there's a minimum of buzzes and rattles, and play. The resulting chord or note will sound higher than the same thing played without the capo. If an E chord is played with the capo clamped on the third fret, the resulting <u>sound</u> will be a G chord, even though the player is holding what looks like an E chord. Each fret is equal to one half step. Since in this case the capo is three frets above the guitar nut, the resulting chord is three half steps above the standard E, which is G. If the capo were on the fourth fret, the resulting chord would become G♯ or A♭.

The practical advantage of the capo is that a guitarist can learn a tune's chord progression or melody in one key and then, by correctly positioning the capo, play that melody or chord progression in several different keys without re-learning it. In this way, you can accommodate your own voice or other singers and players who perform a tune in a different key than you know.

The capo can be an artistic tool as well. Play an open B♭ chord. Now capo at the third fret and play a G chord which now *sounds* like a B♭. Notice the special qualities of each? You may prefer one over the other for a particular effect on a tune. (If you're a beginner, you may find it much easier to play the capoed G than the regular B♭ chord.) When two guitarists work together, one can play open chords while the other plays capoed up. The result is a very full sound. For example, one could play an open C while the other played a G capoed at the fifth fret. Both sound like C with slightly different, though complementary, *voicings*. This is often done on country recordings. One guitarist plays without a capo using open chords, while the other capos as high as possible to get a high, zingy rhythm guitar sound. More on that later.

To determine the new chord, note or key in a capoed position, count up by half steps the number of frets you capo up. The half step or chromatic scale is: C, C♯/D♭, D, D♯/E♭, E, F, F♯/G♭, G, G♯/A♭, A, A♯/B♭, B, C, twelve different notes in all. Notes listed with a slash, like C♯/D♭, are different names, *enharmonic spellings*, for the same note. You can call a note or chord by either name. A G chord capoed up five frets yields the sound of a C chord. What would a G chord be, capoed up six frets? Count half steps/frets up from G:

G	G♯/A♭	A	A♯/B♭	B	C	C♯/D♭
	1	2	3	4	5	6

How about an A chord capoed up one fret?

A	A♯/B♭
	1

The chart following details these relationships. Simply match up the chords you want to hear with the chord you want to play, and place the capo accordingly. Chords are listed with their enharmonic names, for example, an A♯ chord can also be referred to as a B♭ chord. Any chord with these letter names, regardless of suffix, can be used. (For example, C7, Cm, C9, C dim, Cm7, C aug, etc.) Just make sure that you keep the same type chord when you capo. The chart only shows fret numbers to 12 and at that point the whole thing starts all over again. Unless you have an electric guitar with huge gaping cutaways, it's unlikely that you'll capo anywhere near the twelfth fret. You still have to fit your hand in front of the capo! Most guitars won't allow capoing much above the seventh or ninth fret. Guitars will show their unwillingness to be held this tight and this high by playing very out of tune.

Capo Chart

Capo on   *Actual Sound of Chord*

Fret #	1	2	3	4	5	6	7	8	9	10	11	12
C	C♯/D♭	D	D♯/E♭	E	F	F♯/G♭	G	G♯/A♭	A	A♯/B♭	B	C
C♯/D♭	D	D♯/E♭	E	F	F♯/G♭	G	G♯/A♭	A	A♯/B♭	B	C	C♯/D♭
D	D♯/E♭	E	F	F♯/G♭	G	G♯/A♭	A	A♯/B♭	B	C	C♯/D♭	D
D♯/E♭	E	F	F♯/G♭	G	G♯/A♭	A	A♯/B♭	B	C	C♯/D♭	D	D♯/E♭
E	F	F♯/G♭	G	G♯/A♭	A	A♯/B♭	B	C	C♯/D♭	D	D♯/E♭	E
F	F♯/G♭	G	G♯/A♭	A	A♯/B♭	B	C	C♯/D♭	D	D♯/E♭	E	F
F♯/G♭	G	G♯/A♭	A	A♯/B♭	B	C	C♯/D♭	D	D♯/E♭	E	F	F♯/G♭
G	G♯/A♭	A	A♯/B♭	B	C	C♯/D♭	D	D♯/E♭	E	F	F♯/G♭	G
G♯/A♭	A	A♯/B♭	B	C	C♯/D♭	D	D♯/E♭	E	F	F♯/G♭	G	G♯/A♭
A	A♯/B♭	B	C	C♯/D♭	D	D♯/E♭	E	F	F♯/G♭	G	G♯/A♭	A
A♯/B♭	B	C	C♯/D♭	D	D♯/E♭	E	F	F♯/G♭	G	G♯/A♭	A	A♯/B♭
B	C	C♯/D♭	D	D♯/E♭	E	F	F♯/G♭	G	G♯/A♭	A	A♯/B♭	B

Chord held

Capos do have their drawbacks. One is that when moved they usually require you to retune the guitar. I've used just about every type of capo on the market; elastic straps, spring clamps, thumb screw clamps, etc., and they all send your tuning out of whack. That can be a pain in the neck, especially for your audience, if you're on stage and switching positions a lot — you'll spend more time tuning than playing. Another drawback is that capos can become a crutch and a roadblock to learning transposition theory, which we'll get into later in the book. It's also tough to get rid of all the fretboard buzzes and rattles as you move a capo to different positions. Sometimes you just can't get it tight enough to get a good clean sound on every string. I find that the screw-type capo works quite well in these situations. You can torque that baby down to about 300 P.S.I. (Of course if you do, you'll have serious tuning problems and a broken guitar neck.)

The greatest use you'll have for a capo is to change keys to accommodate different singers. If the non-capoed chords are too low or too high, try the capo here and there until you find a key that works better. If I want to play a song that's too low or high for my voice, I usually start by putting the capo on the fourth or fifth fret and work up or down from there, singing a bit at different positions until I find the best one. You can do the same thing with other singers, or if the singer knows what key he or she needs, you can use the chart to figure things out. Here's a demonstration:

Shady Grove was originally presented on page 27 in the key of E minor modal. (Forget for a moment that you're already hip enough to play *Shady Grove* in E minor modal <u>and</u> A minor modal.) Unfortunately, E minor modal is too low for the singer in our band who needs it transposed to A minor modal. How can we use the capo, still play the chords we know in E minor modal, and make everybody happy? Consult the old capo chart! Find the E in the far left column. (Remember to play Em when the time comes.) Follow over to the right horizontally until you find the A. Now follow up in the A column to find out at which fret you have to place the capo. Fret five. So, put your capo on the fifth fret and play the Em and D chords. They'll <u>sound</u> like Am and G! Test it out by playing along with the taped A-minor version of *Shady Grove* while holding the Em chords. Before you do that though, look up the bass notes for the Em and D chords and play bass–strum backup. Someday you'll thank me for all this hard work I'm making you do.

Here's another situation like the one before. You're jamming with another guitarist and just about ready to play *Going Down That Road Feeling Bad*. One serious problem: you know the song in the key of G with the chords G, C, and D7; they know the song in the key of C with the chords C, F, and G. Luckily, being highly intelligent and having access to the capo chart, you have a solution: let your friend play the chords he or she knows in C while you play your chords in G capoed correctly. Find the G chord in the far left column of the capo chart. Follow it over horizontally until you find the column with a C. Follow that column up until you find the fret number, in this case five. There's your solution: you capo at the fifth fret and play the chords you know in G and they'll fit perfectly with your friend's chords uncapoed in C! (Of course, this is assuming that your two guitars are in tune with one another.)

Go back to all the songs you've learned thus far, play them again and practice both strums and flatpick backup with the capo in several different positions on each tune. This is your chance to find a key that fits your voice perfectly. Once you find it, write it in pencil on the sheet music: "Capo 3rd fret/Actual key B♭." You should be forewarned, however, that you won't be able to play along with the recorded versions on the tape. At least for now you won't be able to. We'll show you how later.

.

NINE POUND HAMMER & THE LESTER FLATT RUN

Nine Pound Hammer combines working with a capo, flatpick backup with double strums, connecting runs, and runs based on the Lester Flatt G run we'll tackle on the next tune. First of all, slap your capo on the second fret. Play a G chord. What chord does this *sound* like? Now play the C. What chord does this *sound* like? If you need to, refer back to the capo chart. OK, I'll end the suspense. G chords and C chords played with the capo on the second fret come out sounding like A and D respectively. The D7 will sound like an E7. You'll be capoing up from the key of G to the key of A.

The new run is heard constantly in bluegrass and old time music at the end of phrases. You'll first see it in the backup to the chorus. Here's how it looks on both the G and C chords. Listen to the tape to hear how it sounds.

Counter #: _____

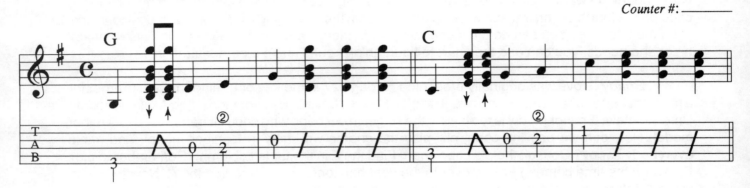

Use double strums throughout *Nine Pound Hammer* in your flatpick backup. Keep in mind, though, that in real life, guitarists rarely play this regularly and will mix up single and double strums, along with whatever else occurs to them at the moment, throughout the course of a song. In the very last measure, I changed the G run to resolve to the G at the third fret of the sixth string. In the example above the run ends on the open third string.

The Nine Pound Hammer

Traditional - Key of G, Capoed 2nd fret = Key of A

Starting note (capoed)

Verse 1. Well the nine pound ham - mer is a lit - tle too hea - vy,
moun - tain, Just to see my ba - by,

Bud - dy for my size, Bud - dy for my size.
And I ain't coming back, Lord I ain't coming back.

Chorus: So roll on bud - dy, Don't you roll so slow,

How can I roll when the wheels won't go? **Verse 2.** I'm go - in' on the

G   C
3. It's a long way to Harlan, it's a long way to Hazard,
          G   D7   G
Just to get a little brew, Just to get a little brew.

4. There ain't no hammer in this tunnel,
That'll ring like mine, That'll ring like mine.

5. I'm working all day, down under ground,
Black as night, it's black as night.

RUNS, UP & DOWN PICKING

The run you just learned is part of a group of very prominent runs widely known as "The G Run" or "The Lester Flatt G Run." Lester Flatt was a guitarist and singer in the bluegrass style. He and banjoist Earl Scruggs played in Bill Monroe's Bluegrass Boys band in the late 1940s, and helped Bill define bluegrass music. They later formed their own very popular band and were often featured on *The Beverly Hillbillies* television show. Lester Flatt's subtle work throughout his career virtually defined the rhythm guitar role in a bluegrass band. There are many variations of the Flatt G run and we'll explore a few. The basic run involves some challenging up-and-down work with the flatpick:

Counter #: _____

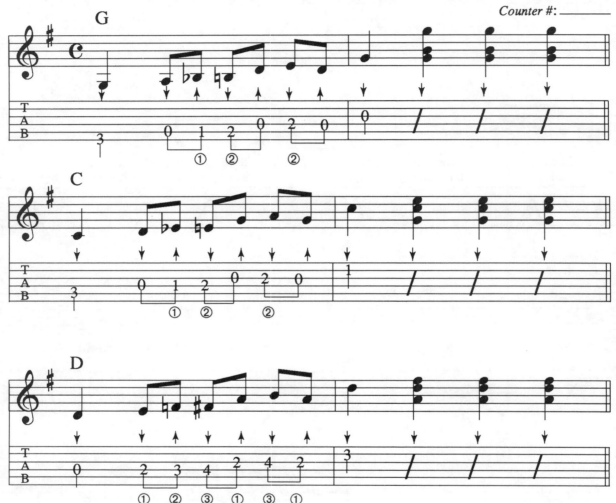

To play this run we need to pick single notes in both up and down directions. You can probably do the downstrokes OK from all the strumming work you've done thus far. The up strokes probably feel very awkward to you and may be difficult to control. Here's an exercise to help with that. Play each string open, first with downstroke quarter notes and then with down-and-up eighth notes. Two eighth notes fit into the time of one quarter note. We count the four quarter notes per measure:

"1 – 2 – 3 – 4,"
↓ ↓ ↓ ↓

and play them with all downstrokes. We count the eight eighth notes per measure:

"1 and - 2 and - 3 and - 4 and,"
↓ ↑ ↓ ↑ ↓ ↑ ↓ ↑

52

and alternate the pick directions down and up. Keep in mind that we're not thinking or playing any faster, rather we're fitting in two eighth notes in the same space where we previously had only one quarter note. We find quarter and eighth notes mixed (often with other notes values, too) and the pick-direction rule that I follow religiously is this: always play downstrokes on beats 1, 2, 3, 4; always play upstrokes on the 'ands.'

Counter #: _____

53

Practice down-up picking constantly. You need to build up the muscles in your hand and help them get coordinated. I hesitate to admit this, but I have mindlessly played the previous exercise, or one similar with all eighth notes, for hours on end, usually in front of the television! (My teachers would horsewhip me for telling you that.) However you do it, it's important to keep the music moving through your fingers.

Here's *Nine Pound Hammer* with several full Lester Flatt runs. Notice that I've changed the G run in measures 9 and 10 (start counting measures after the pickup "Well the nine pound…"), and the C run in measures 11 and 12 to resolve to a note an octave below what you might expect. I also did this in the previous version of *Nine Pound Hammer.*

The Nine Pound Hammer

Melody starting note (capoed)

Traditional - Key of G, Capoed 2nd fret = Key of A

HAMMER-ONS AND PULL-OFFS

Two very useful finger moves in flatpick backup and lead are hammer-ons and pull-offs. (If you're into rap, call them "MC Hammer Ons.") To play them, you pick a note and then, while it's still ringing, "hammer on" or "pull off" with a fretting finger and, hopefully, the picked string will continue to ring and sound the new note. Hammers go from a lower to a higher note, pulls go from higher to lower. Most hammers can be reversed to be pulls and vice versa.

Look at the example below. Hold partial G chord and leave the fifth (A) string open for now. Pick the open A and quickly fret the B (second fret) note on the same string with your second finger (the one you'd normally use to make the full G chord). Practice until both the open A and fretted B notes ring equally well. This may take a bit of practice until the buzzes are eliminated, so don't give up. Try the C-chord example the same way except leave the fourth (D) string open initially and hammer on the second fret.

Counter #: _____

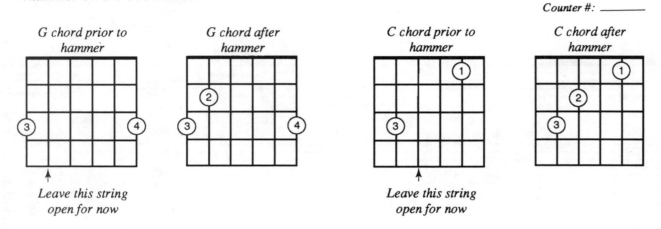

We can create a whole range of different patterns by combining the hammer-on with our basic bass–strum accompaniment. Be sure to hold the complete chord if you have to strum before the hammer-on bass note! Here are a couple patterns:

Counter #: _____

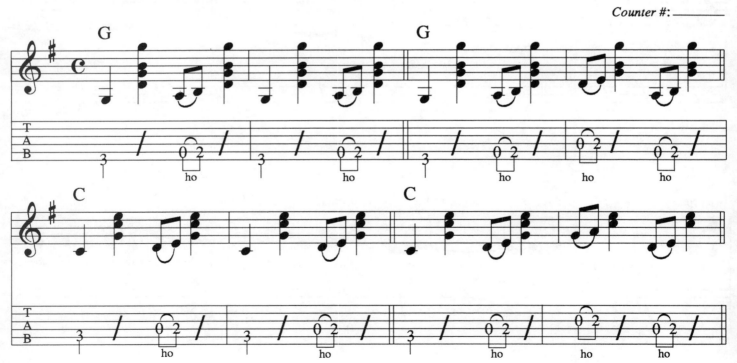

Willie Nelson uses this technique and plays something like it, especially noticeable on the intro in *On the Road Again.* Remember to hold the complete chord for that first strum.

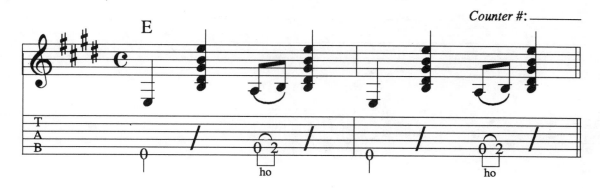

You can add hammers to bass runs:

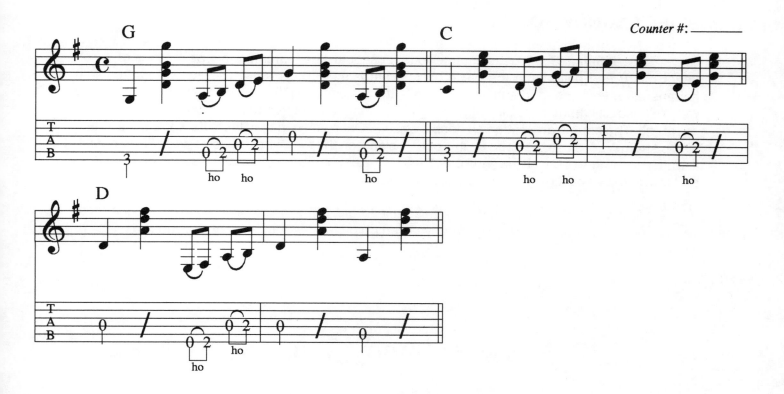

A pull-off is the reverse of a hammer-on. Hold a full G chord and pick the fretted B note (fifth string second fret). Quickly move your fretting finger off the B note and let the open A ring. (The action is probably more of a "push" than a "pull.") I usually push off in the direction of the ceiling, rather than toward the floor. If I'm on the first string, I'll go either way. Again, don't expect it to work perfectly the first time. Try all the above hammer examples with pull-offs.

Other pull-off examples are on the following page.

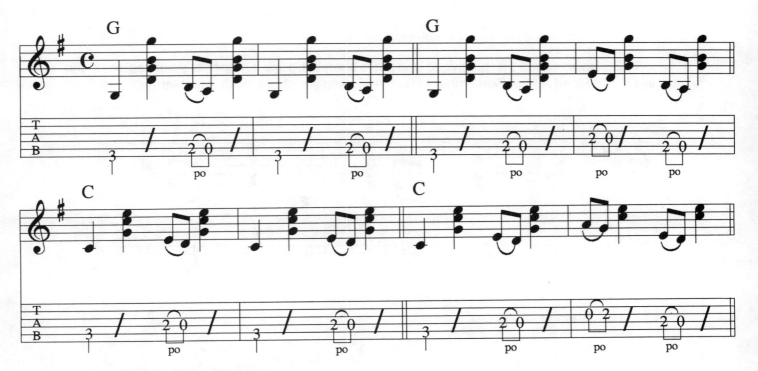

SWEET SUNNY SOUTH

Sweet Sunny South uses hammer-ons (or should it be "hammers-on" as in "sons of ..." oh never mind) and pull-offs in the basic backup and also in bass runs. The song is written with hammers, so you'll need to substitute pull-offs the second time through. In real life you probably wouldn't use all hammers or all pulls throughout a song, so feel free to mix them up or leave them out at will. The strums are written as double strums. Once you can play them as written, substitute single strums. Let's use the capo on this one — slap it on the fourth fret. Since *Sweet Sunny South* is written in the key of C with the chords C, F and G7, can you figure out what the sound of the chords and in what key you'll be if you play the song capoed at the fourth fret?

I first heard *Sweet Sunny South* by Charlie Poole, but Tim and Mollie O'Brien have a great version out on Sugar Hill. Why these guys aren't big country stars is way beyond me—they're wonderful.

Sweet Sunny South

Counter #: _____

Traditional - Key of C, Capoed at 4rd fret = Key of E

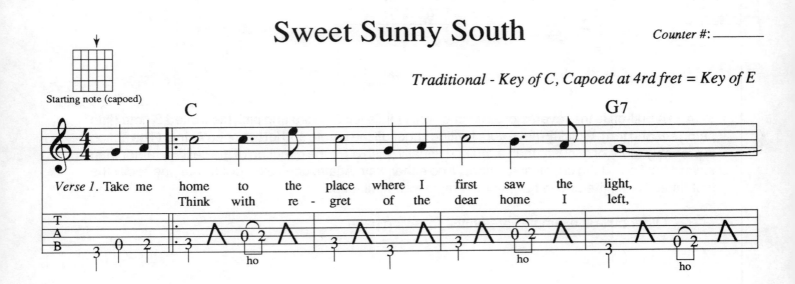

58

3. Take me back to the place where the orange trees grow
To my cot in the evergreen shade.
Where the flowers on the river's green margin may grow
They are sweet on the banks where we played.

4. The path to our cottage they say has gone green
And the place is quite lonely around.
And I know that the smiles and the forms I have seen
Now lie in the dark mossy ground.

5. Take me home, let me see what is left that I knew
Can it be that the old house is gone?
The dear friends of my childhood indeed must be few
And I must lament all alone.

6. But yet I'll return to the place of my birth
Where my children have played at the door.
Where they pulled the white blossoms that garnished the earth
Which will echo their footsteps no more.

Pull-off example (capoed at 4th fret)

Counter #: _____

59

I'LL LOVE YOU STILL

I'll Love You Still will flex your backup capabilities evermore, where you punctuate the vocal phrases with different runs based on everything you've been studying: up and down picking, hammers, pulls, connecting runs, backwards runs, etc. In the third to the last measure I even mixed a pull and hammer in one run! I hope I can play it on the tape!

I'll Love You Still

Counter #: _____

by Dix Bruce - Key of G

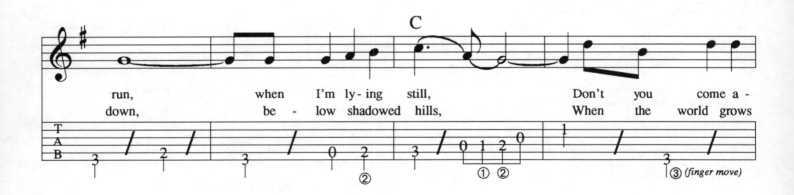

flowers
prayer,

and keep from my
no one will

grave,
hear,

It
For

would

one who's

break

your

G C

G D7 G

heart
gone,

to see me
who loves

this
you

way.
dear.

Chorus: I've known

the

C G

pain

that someday you'll feel,

That emp - ti - ness in -

side

and tears so

real.

Then think of

D A D

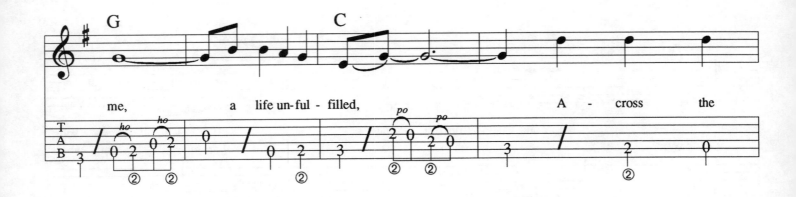

me,   a   life un-ful - filled,   A -   cross   the

years,   I'll   love   you   still.   *to verse 2*

2. When my sun sinks down, below shadowed hills
When the world grows dark and the trees grow still.
Then say a prayer, no one will hear
To one who's gone, who loves you dear.

62

THE NASHVILLE NUMBER SYSTEM

Previously, we explored the use of the capo as a way to change keys and accommodate different pitch ranges of voices. We slap the capo on a given fret, say fret four, and it raises the pitch or sound of the chord we strum by that number, in this case four half steps. Capos offer an easy way to transpose music, but they're ultimately quite limiting: they knock your guitar out of tune, they take time to move, and if you're not careful they can become an obstacle to learning about music theory and getting along without one. Not only that, there are many transposing situations where they won't be of much help.

For example, you're at a Loretta Lynn concert in Branson, MO. Her rhythm guitar player has missed the band bus. The band can't play without him and there's no one in the auditorium who can save the show. The first song on Loretta's set list is *Going Down This Road Feeling Bad*. (Stay with me on this…) "Wait a minute," you think, "I know *Going Down This Road Feeling Bad* in the key of G. I can save the show!" You push your way through the crowd and grab the guitar. The bass player says, "Key of F, kick it off!" "No problem, Slick," you say, "I got my capo in my pocket." Only then do you know that you are doomed. You break out in a cold sweat as you realize there is no way in heaven or hell that you can capo that guitar at the tenth fret. What will you do, WHAT WILL YOU DO? You learn a little music theory, that's what. Read on, fast.

The trick is to look at chords generically and see how they function within a song. As it turns out, the system is very regular and makes perfect sense. Along the way we'll relate it to what is sometimes called "The Nashville Number System," so called because of its use in studios in Nashville to communicate chord progressions among musicians where music is often not written down or read.

When we talked about capos, we used the chromatic scale or half-step scale: C, C♯/D♭, D, D♯/E♭, E, F, F♯/G♭, G, G♯/A♭, A, A♯/B♭, B, C, twelve different notes in all. (You'll recall that notes listed with a slash, like C♯/D♭, are different names, *enharmonic spellings*, for the same note. You won't find notes called E♯/F♭ or B♯/C♭ no matter how long you look. By definition the space between E and F and B and C is one half step. Some know-it-all music Einstein will delight in pointing out that C♭ is really a B natural note and that E♯ is really just an F. Technically true but almost never important in country music.) Notes on adjacent frets follow this chromatic pattern. For example, notes on the first-string E begin with the open E. The first fret note is F, second fret note is F♯/G♭, third fret is G, and so on up to the twelfth fret E, which is an octave higher than the open-string E. Above the twelfth fret, the pattern repeats beginning with the F note at fret thirteen. This is why the capo works the way it does.

We derive our major scale, which most of us know as "do-re-mi-fa-sol-la-ti-do," from the chromatic scale. We can begin this scale on any pitch, any note on the fretboard or keyboard (the first note is always "do"), and find the subsequent notes (re-mi-fa-sol-la-ti-do) by applying a certain set of intervals or distances between each of the notes in the whole-and-half-step pattern shown below. "Wh" stands for *whole step* and "1/2" means *half step*. These intervals define a major scale and a key. The C-major scale has the following notes:

```
          C      D      E      F      G      A      B      C
Scale#  1      2      3      4      5      6      7      8
           wh     wh    1/2    wh     wh     wh    1/2
```

Notice that the 1 and 8 are the same note one octave apart. One half step equals one fret on the guitar, one whole step equals two frets. In a major scale there are whole steps between notes 1 and 2, 2 and 3, 4 and 5, 5 and 6, 6 and 7. There are half steps between notes 3 and 4 and 7 and 8. We number notes in the scale using Arabic numerals and refer to notes in a scale as the "one," "four," "seven," etc.

Now here's the G scale:

	G	A	B	C	D	E	F#	G
Scale#	1	2	3	4	5	6	7	8
		wh	wh	1/2	wh	wh	wh	1/2

There is only one different note from the C major scale, the 7, which had to be raised (sharped) one half step to preserve the half-step interval needed between notes 7 and 8. (Look again at the chromatic scale above if you're not sure where the half steps are.) If we'd left it an F natural note, the interval between notes 7 and 8 would have been a whole step. We'd also have had an incorrect interval of a half step between 6 and 7 where we need a whole step.

You can relate this to the fretboard and play an E-major scale on the first string by ascending the fingerboard with the whole step – half step pattern. Start with the open-string E, go up a whole step or two frets to the second fret F#, two more frets up to fret for G#, etc., to the twelfth fret octave E. Here's what the E-major scale looks like with fret numbers listed below:

	E	F#	G#	A	B	C#	D#	E
Scale#1		2	3	4	5	6	7	8
		wh	wh	1/2	wh	wh	wh	1/2
Fret#	0	2	4	5	7	9	11	12

We build chords and keys on the notes of the major scale. The chords shown below are constructed using only the notes from the major scale, in this case the G-major scale. We're not limited to only these chords, in fact we can change the minors shown to dominant seventh chords, but these are the chords that use only the notes of the major scale. For now, don't worry if you don't see your favorite chords listed below.

Chord#	G	Am	Bm	C	D	Em	F#°	G
	I	ii	iii	IV	V	vi	vii	VIII/I

Chords in keys are labeled with Roman numerals: uppercase for major chords (I, IV, V), lowercase for minor and diminished chords (ii, iii, vi, etc., the seventh is diminished and indicated by °). The VIII and I chords are the same and they name the key. (We refer to notes in a scale as well as chords in a key by numbers. The only difference is context.) The Nashville Number System is all about referring to chords in keys by their Roman numerals rather than by their letter names. This system recognizes that every chord has a certain function within a key: a "I" ("one") a "vi" ("six") a "V" ("five") and so on. So if I tell you that the chord progression to a song is I, IV, V, I, ("one, four, five, one") in the key of C you'll know that I mean to play the chords C, F, G, C. Suppose we need to play the same song in the key of G. The Roman numerals will apply and you'll know to play the chords G, C, D, G. Well, maybe not quite yet! Let's explore this concept more and get back to Loretta — the audience is getting ugly!

You know the chords to *Going Down This Road Feeling Bad* in the key of G and play the chords G, C, and D7. What Roman numerals do we assign to these chords? I, IV, and V. Loretta needs to sing the song in the key of F. What chords will you play? Look at the chart below and swap the I, IV and V chords from the key of F for the I, IV and V chords you know in the key of G.

(Key of G)	G	Am	Bm	C	D	Em	F#°	G
	I	ii	iii	IV	V	vi	vii	VIII/I
(Key of F)	F	Gm	Am	B♭	C	Dm	E°	F

Instead of the G (I) play the F (I), instead of the C (IV) play the B♭ (IV), and instead of the D7 (V) play the C7 (V). The chord suffixes must match so if the V chord is a V7 in the original key, it needs to be a V7 in the transposed key. Look back at *Going Down This Road Feeling Bad* and play it in the key of F. Now get up on that stage and save the show for Loretta! Yeah, I know it's a bit of a fantasy. She probably starts her shows with *Coal Miner's Daughter.* But we can dream, can't we?

DON'T LET YOUR DEAL GO DOWN

Our next song, *Don't Let Your Deal Go Down,* is written in the key of D and uses the chords D, B7, E7, and A7. Here are the chords from the D major scale:

D	Em	F#m	G	A	Bm	C#°	D
I	ii	iii	IV	V	vi	vii	VIII/I

As you'll hear on the tape, D is too low for my voice. I need to sing it in the key of G.

I can hear you already, "Whoa, just a New York minute there buddy! There ain't no B7, or no E7, or even an A7 in that bunch of chords from the D-major scale." Right you are, go to the head of the class! As I mentioned before, these chords (I ii iii etc.) are built using only the <u>naturally occurring</u> notes of the D-major scale, and we can change them if we want. After all, we're musicians. Not only that, we're guitarists! We can do whatever the heck we want! (And in some cases we'll even get away with it!) In the case of this tune, we're going to change the chords from minors to dominant seventh chords. They'll still be six and two chords, they'll just be majors, and instead of using the lowercase Roman numerals which denote minor chords, we'll change them to uppercase to reflect major chords. (Don't worry, the number system will still work no matter what the chord suffixes are as long as we keep them consistent. For example, if our ii chord is a minor seven in one key, it will be a minor seven in the key we transpose to.)

This chord progression, D - B7 - E7 - A7 - D, is known as a "I - VI - II - V - I" ("one - six - two - five - one") chord progression. To play *Don't Let Your Deal Go Down* in a different key, all we have to do is substitute I, VI, II, V, I chords from the new key for the I, VI, II, V, I chords of the original key of D. Look at the example below which we've changed to include dominant seventh chords, instead of the naturally occurring minors. Our I, VI, II, V chord progression from the key of D (chords D, B7, E7, A7) will be changed to G, E7, A7, D7. Write them in pencil on the music over the given chords and try playing along with the tape in the new key of G.

(Key of D)	D	E7	F#7	G7	A7	B7	C#°	D
(Key of G)	G	A7	B7	C7	D7	E7	F#°	G
	I	II	III	IV	V	VI	vii	VIII/I

Don't Let Your Deal Go Down

Starting note

Counter #: _____

Traditional - Key of D

Verse 1. Well I've been all a - round this whole wide world, I've

65

2. When I left my love behind
   B7   E7
She was standing in the door
   A7   D
She threw her arms a- round my neck said
   B7   E7
"Daddy please don't go."
   A7   D

3. Now it's who's gonna shoe your pretty little feet?
Who's gonna glove your hand?
Who's gonna kiss your ruby lips?
Who's gonna be your man?

4. Papa will shoe my pretty little feet,
Mama will glove my hand.
You can kiss my red ruby lips,
When you get back again.

5. Where did you get them high heel shoes,
And the dress that you wear so fine?
Got them shoes from an engineer
Dress from a driver in the mine.

The chart below summarizes all this theory and shows the keys with their naturally occurring chords. To use it, find the horizontal line showing the key of the song you want to transpose. Identify which columns, I, ii, iii, IV, V, etc., the known chords fall in. Then, simply read up or down to the new key and find the transposed chords. Remember that you can change the chords shown below to majors and sevenths as your situation demands it, just like we did with *Don't Let Your Deal Go Down.*

Scale & Transposition Chart

Key	-	Scale → Chord	1 / I	2 / ii	3 / iii	4 / IV	5 / V	6 / vi	7 / vii	8 (1) / VIII (I)
C	none		C	Dm	Em	F	G	Am	B°	C
F	1 - ♭		F	Gm	Am	B♭	C	Dm	E°	F
B♭	2 - ♭		B♭	Cm	Dm	E♭	F	Gm	A°	B♭
E♭	3 - ♭		E♭	Fm	Gm	A♭	B♭	Cm	D°	E♭
A♭	4 - ♭		A♭	B♭m	Cm	D♭	E♭	Fm	G°	A♭
D♭	5 - ♭		D♭	E♭m	Fm	G♭	A♭	B♭m	C°	D♭
G♭	6 - ♭		G♭	A♭m	B♭m	C♭	D♭	E♭m	F°	G♭
C♭	7 - ♭		C♭	D♭m	E♭m	F♭	G♭	A♭m	B♭°	C♭
C#	7 - #		C#	D#m	E#m	F#	G#	A#m	B#°	C#
F#	6 - #		F#	G#m	A#m	B	C#	D#m	E#°	F#
B	5 - #		B	C#m	D#m	E	F#	G#m	A#°	B
E	4 - #		E	F#m	G#m	A	B	C#m	D#°	E
A	3 - #		A	Bm	C#m	D	E	F#m	G#°	A
D	2 - #		D	Em	F#m	G	A	Bm	C#°	D
G	1 - #		G	Am	Bm	C	D	Em	F#°	G

We can transpose songs in minor keys the same way. Let's say we have a song in Em with the chords Em, Am and B7. Use the key-of-E line and think of the I and IV chords as minor, the V as a dominant seventh. Follow the columns up or down to the new key, and make sure you play the new chords appropriately as minors or sevenths. In transposing from the key of Em to the key of Dm, Em becomes Dm, Am becomes Gm, and B7 becomes A7.

The chart will also tell you the notes in all the major scales. Just ignore all the minor and diminished designations. For example, if you read across on the B♭ line you'll see that the B♭ major scale is:

B♭	C	D	E♭	F	G	A	B♭
1	2	3	4	5	6	7	8

Another use for the chart is to determine a song's key. A basic rule of thumb says that most songs end or resolve on the I chord of the key. (If you're on the ball, you'll immediately come up with ten or twenty that don't!) The foolproof way is to look at the key signature on the sheet music and count sharps or flats. Column two of the chart tells which numbers of sharps and flats define which keys. If you can't do that, the chart will still work for transposing a combination of chords — you just might not be sure of which key you're in. Let's say you are playing a song with the chords Am, G, F, and E7. You can't sing it that high so you try substituting an Em for the Am and it's fine. Go to the chart and find an Am in any horizontal line. Follow down to the Em. Find the other chords (G, F, and E7) on the same horizontal line you found the original Am and follow down to the Em line.

Go back to all the previous songs, identify the chords according to their Roman numerals, and write these in pencil above the chord-letter names. Use the chart to practice transposing them, this time without your capo, to other keys and try to find the perfect key in each case for your voice. Train yourself to think of chords by their numerical designations, not their alphabetical names. This will allow you to put theory into practice as you begin to understand the relationships between chords and keys. You'll also find it easier to communicate with other musicians and open yourself up to unknown worlds of music. Most pop, folk, country, rock, and bluegrass songs tend to follow one of a handful of standard chord progressions. Musicians can indicate these quickly, clearly, and easily in one phrase like "one, five," "one, five, one, four, one, five, one," or "one, six, two, five." You'll also find that numbers like "one, six, two, five" shouted across a stage in a noisy bar will be much more easily understood than the sound-alikes "Geeeee!, Eeeeee!, Aaaaay!, Deeeee!" That's the story on the Nashville Number System. It may take you a while to think numbers instead of letters, but I guarantee your time will be well spent.

CHILDREN GO WHERE I SEND THEE

Let's get back to flatpicking for a minute and look at *Children Go Where I Send Thee*. The accompaniment is written out with an intro and a nice bluesy descending run on the E chord. I remember singing this as a kid, but I love Ricky Skaggs' version with its great fingerpick backup.

Children Go Where I Send Thee

Counter #: _____

Starting note of melody

Traditional - Key of E

Intro vamp/lick

go where I send thee, How shall I send thee?

I'm a gon - na send thee one by one, One for the lit - tle bit - ty ba - by was
two by two, Two for Joseph and Ma - ry,
three by three, Three for the three old wise men,

born, born, born in Beth - le - hem. Chil - dren

(To 2nd staff)

* 1st X– no repeat, go on; 2nd X– repeat, go on; 3rd X– repeat twice, go on; etc.

4. Four by four, four for the four who stood at the door
5. Five by five, five for the Hebrew children
6. Six by six, six for the six who couldn't get fixed.
7. Seven by seven, seven for the seven who wouldn't get to heaven
8. Eight by eight, eight for the eight who stood at the gate.

JOSHUA FOUGHT THE BATTLE OF JERICHO, FINGER MOVES ON MINOR CHORDS, MORE TRANSPOSING

You've already worked with moving your finger to play bass notes with strums on major chords. You can do the same on many of the minor chords. Let's look at the familiar *Joshua Fought the Battle of Jericho* and exercise both our bass-playing fingers and our new knowledge of transposing. We'll start out with the song in the key of F minor. The good news is that it only has two chords, im and V7 or Fm and C7. The bad news is that the Fm is a little tough to play. Here they are diagrammed to show fingerings and bass-note moves:

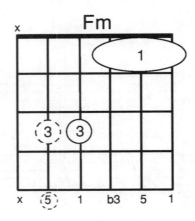

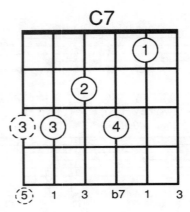

Here's *Joshua Fought the Battle of Jericho.* By the way, this sign: ✗ means to repeat what you played in the previous measure.

Joshua Fought the Battle of Jericho

Traditional - Key of Fm

Starting note

2. Up to the walls of Jericho he marched with his spear in his hand,
"Go blow those ram horns," Joshua cried "'cause the battle is in my hands."

3. Then the ramhorns began to blow, the trumpets began to sound,
Joshua commanded the children to shout and the walls came tumbling down.

As you can see, it's pretty much the same thing as you did on the major chords. Let's try transposing to another minor key – how about G minor? You already know what the im will be – Gm. How about the V7? Check the transposition chart, or cheat and look below. (Remember, you'll only be hurting yourself!)

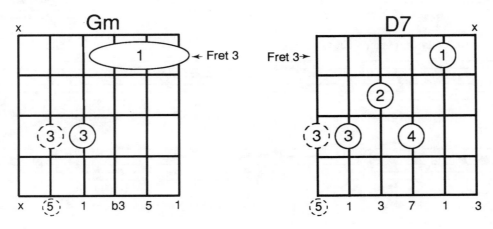

Here's where it gets very interesting. (Expect a light bulb to go on in your head over this next bit.) Look how similar the Fm and Gm are. Same with the C7 and D7. All are closed-position chords. When we have closed-position or *barre* chords with all fretted and no open strings, we can move them to any fret on the guitar neck and easily play several different chords. In the case of *Joshua*, we moved the whole thing up, lock, stock, and barrel, two frets. We know from our previous work that two frets equal one whole step, and that one whole step above F is G. It's just like having a built-in capo. Of course it's very important to observe which strings are muted with the fretting hand. Suddenly with the D7, we can't let the first-string E note ring as we did with the C7 because the E is not part of the D7 chord. It'll take a good bit of practicing to play these types of chords cleanly, so be patient. Write in the new chords in pencil and play *Joshua* in Gm.

Once you can play it G minor, move the whole thing up one more fret. Suddenly you're playing in G♯minor/A♭ minor. Now move the whole thing down two frets and play in F♯minor/G♭ minor. Ain't music grand? Now let's look at another moveable form, the Cm, and play *Joshua* once more in C minor. Again, the Cm is moveable up and down the fingerboard. Remember to observe the muted strings. You'll also see a closed position G7 below.

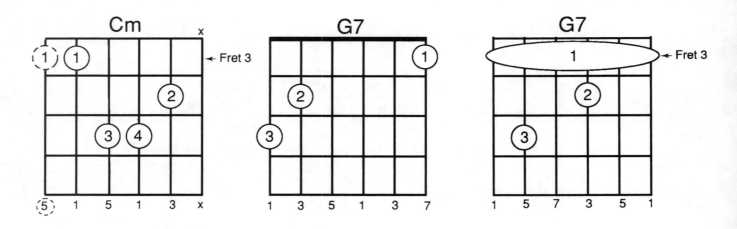

FINGERPICKING

Everything you've learned so far has been done with a flatpick. But there's plenty of guitar work in country music with naked fingers. I especially like the backup on some of the Judds' CDs. Check the chart on page 91 and make sure you know where the bass notes (usually the one and the five of the chord) are on the E, A, and B7 chords. (You had this same combination of chords on *Red River Valley*.) The pattern is played slowly on the tape, and the E chord is diagrammed below. Hold the regular E chord with your fretting hand. With your other hand, pick downward on the sixth-string low E with the thumb, and then pick upward with first your index finger on the fourth string, then your middle finger on the third, and finally your ring finger on the second string. The pattern is "thumb, index, middle, ring" and is often referred to as an arpeggio pick. These moves are diagrammed below:

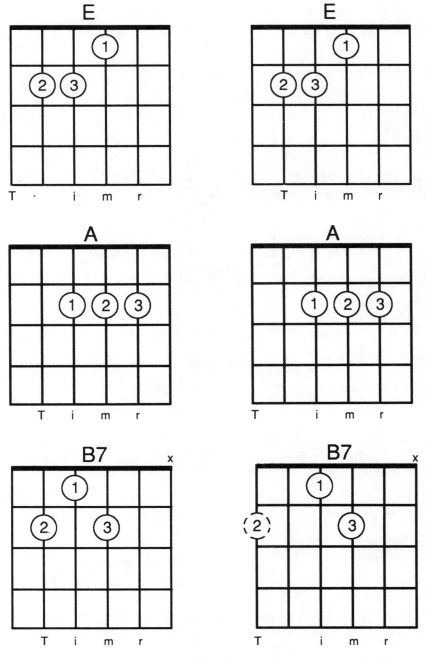

"Partial" B7 chords

73

You'll do the same thing with the A and B7 chords. Notice the "partial" B7 chord. Usually, you'd fret the first string second fret with your fourth finger, but since you don't play the first string in this pattern, you don't need to fret it. This is good news to me with my big fat fingers, as I sometimes have trouble getting the second string to ring cleanly when my fourth finger is on the first string.

Don't This Road Look Rough & Rocky?

Counter #: _____

Traditional - Key of E

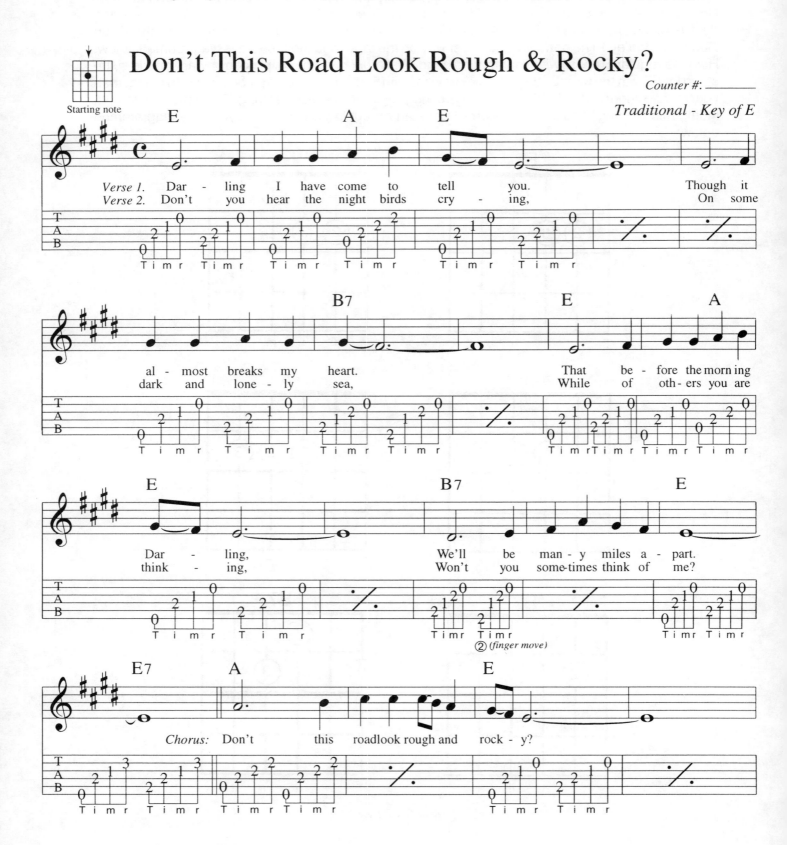

Verse 1. Darling I have come to tell you. Though it
Verse 2. Don't you hear the night birds cry - ing, On some

al - most breaks my heart. That be - fore the morn ing
dark and lone - ly sea, While of oth - ers you are

Darling, We'll be man - y miles a - part.
think - ing, Won't you some-times think of me?

② (finger move)

Chorus: Don't this roadlook rough and rock - y?

74

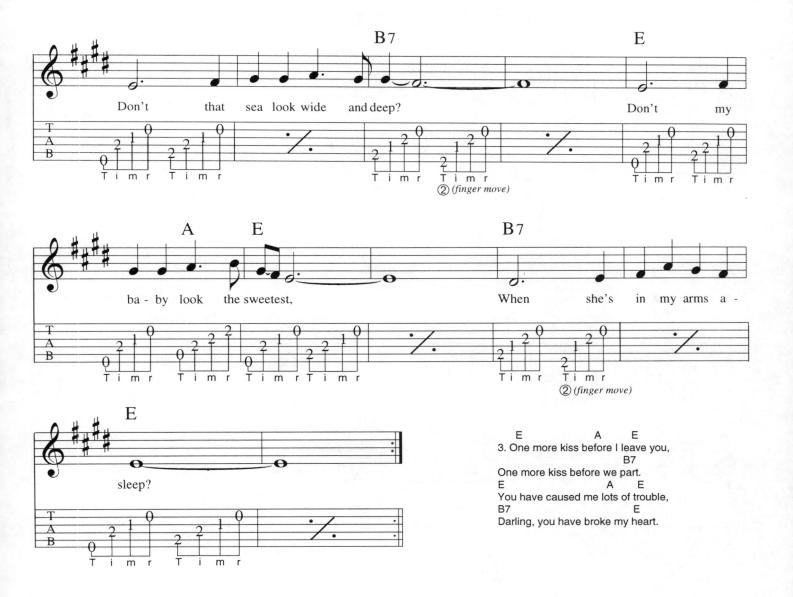

FAIR & TENDER LADIES

Fair & Tender Ladies is another song with a finger pattern. The only tricky part is that you have to move a finger, just like you did with the basic flatpick backup, to play the other bass note on the C chord. See the diagram below:

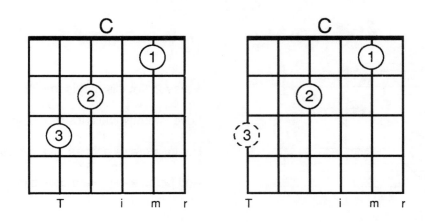

Fair & Tender Ladies

Traditional - Key of C

Verse 2: Love is handsome, love is charming,
Love is pretty while it's new,
But love grows cold as love grows older,
And fades away like morning dew.

76

DOUBLE ARPEGGIO FINGERPICK, IN THE PINES

In the Pines uses sort of a double arpeggio — you play the bass note with your thumb, then the same type of arpeggio pick as *Don't This Road Look Rough & Rocky,* "thumb, index, middle, ring" for the first part, then middle and index again. Here's how it looks on the D chord in tablature:

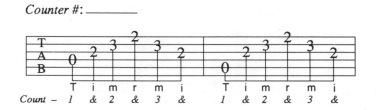

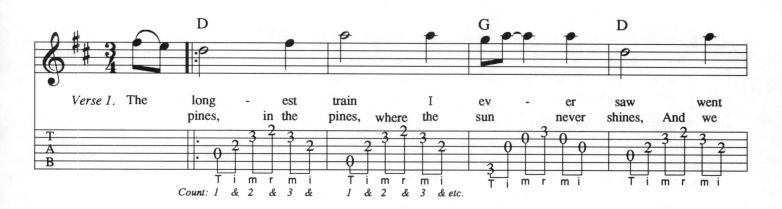

This pattern works best on songs in 3/4 time, waltzes like *Old Paint, Home on the Range,* etc. Garth Brooks uses something like this on his *Night Rider's Lament.* The chords, D, G, and A7, should be quite familiar to you. Have at it!

In the Pines

Traditional - Key of D

2. I asked my captain for the time of day
                                 A7   D
He said he'd thrown his watch a- way.
                               G   D
It's a long steel rail and a short cross tie
                D   A7   D
I'm on my way back home.

3. Little girl, little girl, what have I done
To make you treat me so?
You've caused me to weep you've caused me to mourn
You've caused me to leave my home.

Another great finger pattern is based on the flatpick bass-note strum pattern you already know – you just don't need a flatpick. All you do is substitute the picking-hand thumb for the flatpick on alternating bass notes, and a three-finger pick for the strum. Use the same three picking-hand fingers on the same three strings as above, same bass notes, etc., but instead of picking the strings individually, pick them all at once. Check it out on the tape on *In the Pines* and *Don't That Road Look Rough & Rocky?* Try it on both 4/4 and 3/4 tunes and practice them on all the previous tunes by playing along with the tape.

THE HOUSE OF THE RISING SUN

The same fingerpicking pattern from above works well on the old song, *The House of the Rising Sun.* Part of it is written out in tablature below. See if you can finish the rest. Also try this flatpick strum /∧ /// which is a combination of two different 3/4 strums: /∧ and ///. I'm sure you've heard the hit version of this song by the Animals from the '60s. This more traditional version is from a woman's point of view, and I think very powerful and moving.

It has probably occurred to you that you can shift your fingers to other sets of strings, or play the strings in different orders, for example, instead of T, string 4, 3, 2, you could play T, string 3, 2, 1; T, string 4, 2, 3; or any other combination you can think of. You can also connect these fingerpicked chord patterns with bass runs and connectors played with your thumb. You might have to abbreviate your arpeggio pick somewhat to fit it all in. Try it!

The House of the Rising Sun

Traditional - Key of Am/C

Am   C   D

3. Go tell my baby sister
Am   C   E7
Not to do what I have done
Am   C   D   F
Shun that house in New Orleans
Am   E7   A
They call the Rising Sun.

4. One foot on the platform
The other's on the train
I'm going back to New Orleans
To wear that ball and chain.

5. Going back to New Orleans
My race is almost run
I'm going to spend the rest of my life
Beneath that Rising Sun.

NOBODY SLEEPS AT MY PLACE

Before we get into lead flatpicking, let's take one more look at a very important strum. If you listen carefully to a lot of current country music, you'll find it everywhere; The Judds' *Girl's Night Out* or *Why Not Me*, Merle Haggard's *If We're Not Back in Love By Monday*, Dwight Yoakam's *I Got You*, Mary Chapin Carpenter's *Too Tired*, George Strait's *Fool Hearted Memory* and *All My Ex's Live in Texas*. Dwight Yoakam's and Buck Owens' *Streets of Bakersfield*, almost a Mexican polka, is perfect for hearing the feel of this accompaniment. I call it the backbeat strum, and it's just a little tricky because you rest on the downbeats (beats one and three) and play on the off beats (beats two and four). The tendency is to wander a little bit, because you don't have that downbeat to even it all out. Think of it as a bass–strum pattern without the bass notes! Here's what it looks like:

```
 ᕤ       /       ᕤ       /       |
 1       2       3       4
rest   strum    rest   strum
```

The symbols on beats one and three denote rests. If I find myself drifting on the strums, I tap my foot on all four beats and imagine my foot to be the bass note I'm leaving out. You can also strum or play the root note of the chord lightly to keep yourself honest, and if you listen to similar strums on CDs, you'll hear the downbeats just barely played or played and muffled so the backbeat is still king. In a band situation, you'll need to key in on the bass player or the drummer's bass drum to make it all work. You could also think of this strum overlaid on a two-beat scheme counted "1 and 2 and I 1 and 2 and" with your rests on beats 1 and 2, single up-strums on the "ands." Again, keep in mind that in the real world most strums are not adhered to strictly. Feel free to add downbeats or "and" strums if you get the feel.

This holds true for all the strums and picks you've learned — they can all be customized infinitely and you should experiment to find new and interesting ways of changing them. Just to put these possibilities into a realistic context keep in mind that almost every song you play will be in 4/4 or 3/4 time. You'll recall that you can play all straight downstrums (/ / / / etc.), all down-and up-strums (∧ ∧ ∧ ∧ etc.), you can mix singles and doubles, and you can leave out the up-strums here and there. George Strait does that on *Amarillo By Morning* with the pattern "down–up, down–up, up, down." Mary Chapin Carpenter's *Slow County Dance* starts with a nice "bass note, strum, strum" pattern. Emmy Lou Harris' *Making Believe* uses sort of a "bass, /, bass \ /" thing, while here *Hello Stranger* is straight Carter backup "bass, /, alt. bass, /." You can combine two or more whole patterns, even combine strums with bass–strum backup. The sky's the limit!

Nobody Sleeps has a new type of chord, the diminished chord. You won't find it that often in country music, but every once in a while it crops up. And, it's a great chord. Any note in the chord can name it (this is also C, A, and E♭ diminished seven). This form, having no open notes, can be moved all over the neck. Also, and this is really great, it's the same chord if you move it up three frets, six frets, nine frets, or twelve frets.

You'll notice that *Nobody Sleeps* has a chord progression in the key of C, similar to *Don't Let Your Deal Go Down*. That's right, it's a I VI II V progression. In time, you'll be able to recognize chord progressions from hearing them, and this may be one of the hardest. When you hear a new song, try to play along and listen for the changes. Try every chord you can think of until you find one that sounds right. When you're stumped, consult the sheet music. It may take a while to develop, but trial and error is the best teacher for chord progressions. By the way, *Nobody Sleeps* is the other song I wrote especially for this book. I hope you dig it. I just heard Randy Travis' *Oh What a Time to Be Me,* and it combines a type of country swing backup with a modified backbeat strum, kind of like what I'm going for on *Nobody Sleeps*.

Nobody Sleeps at My Place

by Dix Bruce, Key of C

Counter #: _____

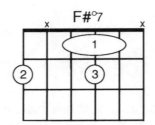

No-bod-y sleeps   at   my place,   Not the   dog, not the cat, not me.   We're
No-bod-y eats   at   my place,   Not the   dog, not the cat, not me.

up   all night,   Walk-ing   the floor,   Miss-ing   your sweet   com-pan - y.
Somehow we lost   our   app - e - tite,   And we just   ain't hun - gry. When a

Toe-nails click-ing   on the   kit-chen floor,   Tongues hang-ing   out about a   mile or more.
dog won't eat   and a   cat won't sleep,   Better dig a   hole and   dig it deep.

No-bod-y sleeps   at   my place,   Not the   dog, not the cat, not me.
No-bod-y eats   at   my place,   Not the   dog, not the cat, not me.

C   A7
3. Everybody howls at my place
D7   G7   C
The dog, the cat, and me.
C   A7
We take a deep breath and let it fly
D7   G7
In three-part harmony.

C   C7
If you love this dog and if you love this cat
F   F#°
Come on home and we'll end this spat
C   A7
Everybody howls at my place
D7   G7   C
The dog, the cat, and me.

CARTER-STYLE LEADS, WILDWOOD FLOWER

Grab that pick once again and we'll work on playing leads on a couple of tunes. *Wildwood Flower* demonstrates a technique pioneered by the great Mother Maybelle Carter of the famous Carter Family and often called "Carter-style" picking. This technique allowed her to play melody notes and punctuate them with strums to fill in the rhythm. The technique is very effective in small groups where the guitar is the main rhythm instrument. If the guitar drops out to play a lead, the rhythm can fall apart. Think of Carter picking as a kind of extension of the type of flatpick backup you've been working with. *Wildwood Flower* is just a little more complex than straight backup with a few extra notes added, some of them hammer-ons. All the strums are shown as single down-strums. Try it also with double down-up strums. Mix them up. Listen to the tape and play along. Once you can play it as written, substitute pull-offs for the hammers. If you're interested in learning more about this style, check out my book/tape set *Beginning Country Guitar Handbook* from Mel Bay Publications. The title is sort of inaccurate, it was originally written as a beginning flatpick book. This type of flatpicking is examined in depth along with the type of lead flatpicking explored in the next tune, *Devil's Dream.*

Wildwood Flower

Traditional - Key of G

LEAD FLATPICKING, DEVIL'S DREAM

Unlike *Wildwood Flower*, *Devil's Dream* is straight hot lead picking. *Devil's Dream* was originally a fiddle tune, and it's anyone's guess what devils dream about. (Probably a government job in Washington!) Playing fiddle tunes on the guitar was pioneered by giants like Doc Watson, Clarence White, Dan Crary, Tony Rice, and Norman Blake. You'll need to refresh your memory on straight up-and-down picking. Quarter notes are generally played as downstrokes. Eighth notes are played down or up depending upon where in the measure they fall: downstrokes on beats 1, 2, 3, 4, upstrokes on the "ands." See the detailed excerpt below.

Counter #: _____

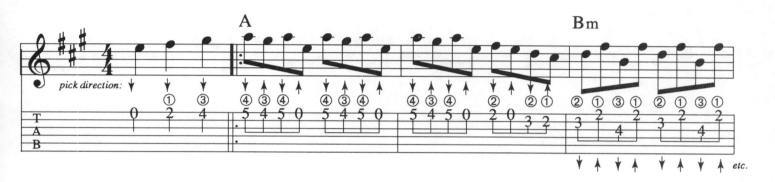

I marked a few spots in the excerpt above where you might get confused about pick direction. Take it very slow at first and give your brain and hands a chance to adjust. The technique you'll be using here is quite advanced, so make it easy on yourself and give yourself time. If you'd like to work more on playing fiddle tune-type leads, try my book/tape set *Back Up Trax: Old Time and Fiddle Tunes, Vol. 1*. It teaches a bunch of the most popular tunes in the repertoire, and the tape is basically a rhythm section of guitar, mandolin, and bass to back you up as you practice. Backup and melody are provided at slow speed plus regular speed with the band. *Devil's Dream* is scheduled to be in volume two. You can hear a preview of the regular speed/band version on the tape.

Devil's Dream

Traditional - Key of A

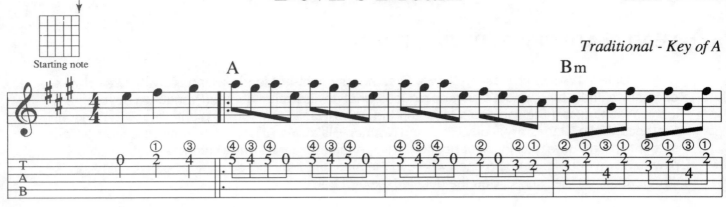

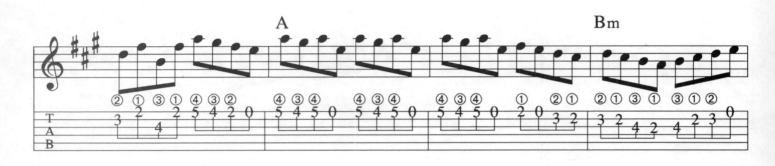

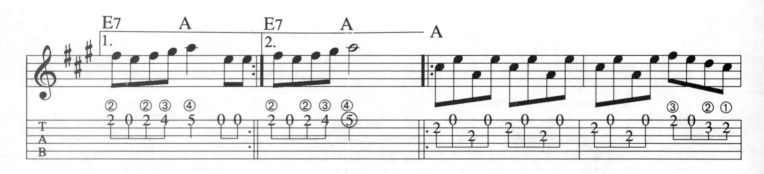

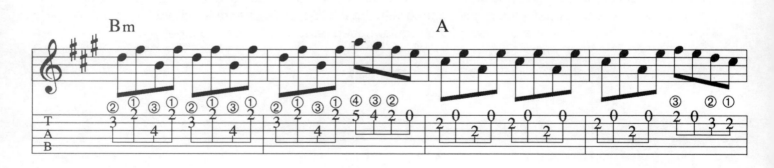

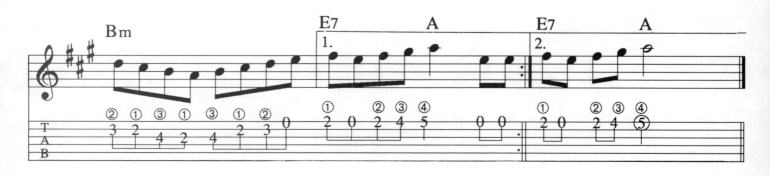

DARLING YOU'RE A FOOL

Darling You're a Fool features a bit of advanced backup with descending lines. It's a bit like the backup scheme for Jerry Jeff Walker's *Mr. Bojangles*. The tablature says it all. I like to sing it in the key of E♭, though to get the bass notes, I still play it out of C position capoed at the third fret.

Darling, You're a Fool

Counter #: _____

by Dix Bruce - Key of C, Capoed 3rd fret = Key of Eb

Verse 1. Dar - ling you're a fool to leave me, A fool to
can't cheat a cheat - er, Or lie to a

run a - way and leave me now.
li - ar for ve - ry long.

When I don't know how to hold you, I don't know how to
Or steal from a thief, Have some - thing left to

hold you or let you be.
keep that's worth it all.

may - be   I'm the fool
you   can   love this lover,   for   try - ing   to   love   you.
                                            who's   do - ing his best   to love   you.

C/b   Am   G
                    1.   2.
                            You

ENDS AND BEGINNINGS

Photo by Rob Thomas

Well, here we are at the end of the book, which really is just a beginning for you. We've explored an overview of chords, strums, songs, flatpicking, fingerpicking, music theory, the Nashville Number System, and more, all designed to get you up and picking country. And, when you've mastered the concepts in this book, you'll be able to back up singers or play in bands. Be patient though, it takes time: hours of practice, hundreds of jam sessions, lots of gigs playing in front of uninterested crowds, dropping your pick, forgetting words, not getting paid, etc. The important thing to remember is that you survive it all, grow stronger from the difficult parts, and if you have the muse deep inside of you, you'll find that you almost *have* to play. I hope the elementary tools you've worked with in this book will help in that endeavor.

So, what's ahead? Just about anything you can think of. What you've seen here is just the slightest surface scratched of a vast musical world of chords, lead flat–and fingerpicking, backup playing, etc. There are thousands more chords and picking patterns, lead and backup, and millions of ways to put them altogether as music. With the knowledge and skills you're developing now, you can help forge the future of country music. You may be the hot Nashville cat of tomorrow. Maybe you'll play locally at clubs and parties. Maybe you'll play at home for friends and family. You may become a writer; a rich one, a struggling one, or one who just writes for the creative urge. All are equally valid, and the important point is to keep playing and have fun shaking hands with the muse inside of you every once in awhile. Write to me with your comments and jokes c/o Musix, PO Box 231005, Pleasant Hill, CA 94523.

CHORD DICTIONARY

Major Chords

| E | A* | D | G | C |

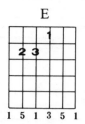
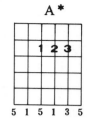
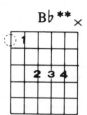
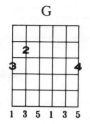
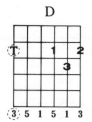

Alternate Fingering

| F | Bb ** | B♮ | * A | ** Bb |

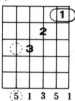
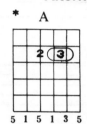
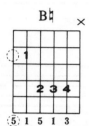
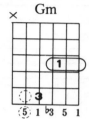
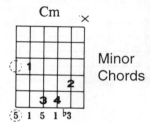

Minor Chords

| Em | Am | Dm | Gm | Cm |

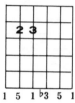
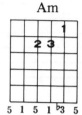
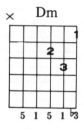
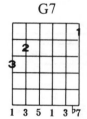
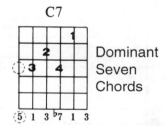

| Fm | Bbm | B♮m |

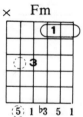
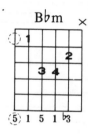
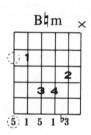

Dominant Seven Chords

| E7 | A7 | D7 | G7 | C7 |

| F7 | Bb7 | B7 |

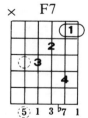
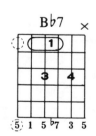
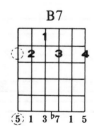
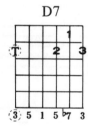

◌ Finger must move to play
× String should't be played

Note: There are often many ways to make given chords and different forms to use. These are the most basic. For further study, find a good chord dictionary.